This book is to be returned on or before the last date below.
THANK YOU FOR USING YOUR LIBRARY

This book is to be returned on or before the last date below.
You may renew the book unless it is requested by another borrower.
You can now renew your books by phone or on-line
visit our website www.libraries.sandwell.gov.uk
THANK YOU FOR USING YOUR LIBRARY

ALBION MEMORIES

ALBION MEMORIES

Express & Star

Breedon Books
Publishing Company
Derby

First published in Great Britain by
The Breedon Books Publishing Company Limited
Breedon House, 44 Friar Gate, Derby, DE1 1DA.
1998

ISBN 1 85983 143 5

Printed and bound by Butler & Tanner Ltd., Selwood Printing Works, Caxton
Road, Frome, Somerset.

Colour separations by Freelance Repro, Leicester.

Jackets printed by Lawrence-Allen, Avon.

Contents

Foreword

WE at the *Express & Star* are proud to be associated with this quality publication on West Bromwich Albion, one of the major clubs in our circulation area.

For decades, the paper has covered Albion's fortunes diligently; this lengthy tribute to the club is an extension to that service and sound working relationship.

The *Express & Star* picture library has formed a considerable part of this book, many of the photographs having been taken by the paper's experienced Head of Pictures, Geoff Wright, and more latterly by Sandwell-based Paul Turner.

We are also greatly indebted to Albion historian and author Tony Matthews, who has generously made his massive photograph collection available to us. He has already written around 30 books – more than half of them on Albion - and we trust we have left enough of his archive material untouched for his planned future publications! Tony's diligence with proof-reading has also been extremely valuable.

Albion, in particular secretary Dr John Evans, have also been highly co-operative, notably with allowing the 'raiding' of framed old photographs on their guest-room walls.

Finally, there have been numerous donated items from Albion supporters and collectors, among them Laurie Rampling, Barry Marsh, Alan Cleverly, Kevin Grice, Michael Reynolds, Terry Wills, Barry Swash, Pat Jordan, Dean Walton, Ian Townsend, Mark Meddings, Denis Clarebrough, Paul Joannou, Ken Coton and Mike Thomas, plus various other *Express & Star* readers. Their help is also much appreciated.

We hope they and the club feel this book is a worthy tribute to Albion's proud history.

The *Express & Star* have now produced quality pictorial histories on Albion and Wolves while Breedon Books have a long and distinguished history in producing such works. If you have any old photographs of these two neighbour clubs and are willing to lend them for possible inclusion in future books, please send them to Memories, Sports Desk, Express & Star, 51-53 Queen Street, Wolverhampton, West Midlands, WV1 3ES. If readers have old pictures of any other clubs for the same purpose, please address them to The Editor, Breedon Books, Breedon House, 44 Friar Gate, Derby, DE1 1DA. All photographs will be returned safely within a few days and will be acknowledged in any publication in which they are used.

Introduction

WEST Bromwich Albion may be into their second decade of life outside the top flight of English football. But those lean years don't mask the club's place among the proud, well-established names of the game in this country.

Founder members of the Football League back in 1888, they made their mark early with FA Cup triumphs in the same year and in 1892 and with three losing appearances in the Final before the turn of the century

Another Final outing came in 1912, still in the pre-Wembley days, followed by the glory of Football League championship success in 1919-20.

Albion made history in 1931 by becoming the first (and so far only) club to win promotion to the top flight and the FA Cup in the same season, finishing as Cup runners-up again four years later.

Britain's post-war era brought the club another wave of success and, of all clubs, neighbours Wolves got in the way when Albion appeared destined to do the double under the managership of Vic Buckingham in 1953-54. The Cup duly ended up back at The Hawthorns but it was at Molineux that the championship came to rest after a dramatic April swing in the balance of power between the two neighbouring clubs.

It was in the Cups – by now there were two domestic knockouts – that Albion made such a thrilling impression the following decade, with journeys to four Finals, and one other semi-final, in five years.

Victorious in 1965-66 in the League Cup in the last year that its Final was played over two legs, Jimmy Hagan's side then lost at the twin towers in the same competition the following year.

It was back to Wembley just over a year later, this time under Alan Ashman and in the more auspicious environment of the FA Cup. And the occasion was a triumphant one as Albion defied the odds to defeat 1966 winners Everton.

European competition and tours to exotic points of the globe came with the club's successes, although the League Cup Final defeat against Manchester City in 1970 was to prove Albion's last appearance at Wembley for 23 years.

In the meantime, their proud span of almost a quarter of a century as a top-flight club was ended by relegation – a drop they reversed three years later after Johnny Giles had become their first-ever player-manager.

And the return to the big league brought a flirt both with the title and European glory in 1978-79, Ron Atkinson's side finishing an unflattering third behind Liverpool and Nottingham Forest and narrowly going out in the quarter-final of the UEFA Cup.

FA Cup semi-finals in 1978 and 1982 marked the end of the dizzy times, for now, for the club, who, with a swish redeveloped ground and a new constitution, plc and all, are busily striving for promotion and a fresh foothold in the game.

Their contribution to English football has been substantial. Both in terms of five FA Cup triumphs, one League Cup success, a League title win, spirited European progress – and big-name personnel.

Great players have come out of The Hawthorns: Bassett, W. G. Richardson, Allen, Barlow, Nicholls, Howe, Astle, Brown, Regis to name but a few. Then there have been the numerous off-field loyal club stalwarts, typified by the father-son Everiss succession – Fred as secretary-manager in the first half of the century and Alan later on. Incredibly, the family duo have spanned the whole of the 20th century with their magnificent service.

West Bromwich Albion are a club packed with tradition and pride. Enjoy this pictorial journey through their history.

Early Days

Stripes everywhere but not a net to be seen! The umpire keeps a close eye on proceedings at the far post as Albion's Jem Bayliss heads for goal during his club's FA Cup Final against Villa at Kennington Oval in 1887. It was the second successive year Albion had been defeated in the Final. The club had lost to Blackburn in a replayed Final in 1885-86.

Albion's first team of FA Cup winners. The Oval was the venue as this side beat Preston 2-1 in the 1887-88 Final after defeating Wednesbury Old Athletic, Mitchell's St George, Wolves, Stoke, Old Carthusians and Derby Junction en route. Albion had a bye in round four of their first victorious year. Back row (left to right): A. Aldridge, E. Horton, H. Green, G. Timmins, R. Roberts, C. Perry, J. Wilson. Front: G. Woodhall, W. Bassett, J. Bayliss, T. Pearson.

Cup winners again. There's a casual, almost nonchalant look from the side who defeated Aston Villa 3-0 in the Final back at The Oval on April 2, 1892, with goals from Geddes, Nicholls and Reynolds. Old Westminsters were among the clubs Albion beat on their way to glory. Pictured are (left to right): W. Bassett, M. Nicholson, J. Reynolds, R. McLeod, J. Reader, S. Nicholls, C. Perry, T. Pearson, W. Groves, T. McCulloch, J. Geddes.

Albion (light shirts) about to concede their first goal in a 3-1 First Division defeat at Notts County on September 6, 1902.

A young Fred Everiss, who, with his son Alan, was to give Albion combined service of more than 100 years, appears on this 1905-06 team picture. Fred, far right on the back row, later became manager as well as secretary – the post he held at this time. Also shown are (back row from left): W. Bassett (director), W. Barber (trainer), J. Pennington, G. Young, J. Stringer, A. Adams, A. Randle. Middle: F. Haycock, C. Simmons, E. Pheasant, F. Shinton, A. Haywood, E. Perkins. Front: E. Bradley, W. Law.

FA Cup Final day, 1912. Extra-time couldn't separate Albion and Barnsley in a goalless deadlock at Crystal Palace in front of a crowd of 55,213, many of whom took to standing on chairs so they could see from the back! The Yorkshire club had something approaching home advantage for the replay at Sheffield and won 1-0.

No way through! Albion 'keeper Hubert Pearson punches clear a Tottenham corner as Billy Minter challenges him during the League clash at White Hart Lane on September 9, 1911. Albion lost 1-0 – their only defeat in a five-game start to the First Division season in which they won their other four matches. Later in the campaign, Albion beat Spurs 3-0 at The Hawthorns at the outset of their run to the FA Cup Final.

Villa Park victors. Albion had no trouble overcoming their local rivals in this First Division away game on September 21, 1912. A hat-trick from striker Bob Pailor, who ended this and the previous season as the club's leading scorer, saw Villa off to the tune of 4-2. The fixture traditionally proved a crowd-puller, this attendance of 55,064 standing as the biggest Albion had played in front of in the League at the time.

Between Two Wars

Round the post. Albion goalkeeper Hubert Pearson touches away a Charlton effort during a 1-0 FA Cup third-round defeat at The Valley in 1922-23.

FA Cup time again. Bramall Lane is the setting as Albion's George Shaw clears from a grounded position as skipper Fred Reed looks on during the 2-0 fourth-round defeat against Sheffield United in March, 1925. Football's boom-time was reflected in another massive gate of 57,197.

Feet on the ground. Albion skipper Fred Reed remains rooted to the spot as he is beaten by an airborne opponent in the First Division game at Bolton in October, 1925. This 2-2 draw came during a high-scoring run for the Baggies. The week before, they crushed West Ham 7-1 at The Hawthorns and, shortly afterwards, drew 4-4 at home to Notts County and beat visiting Bury 4-0.

On the way to Wembley! Albion's Tommy Glidden challenges as Tottenham 'keeper Spiers punches clear in Spurs' 1-0 FA Cup fourth-round defeat at The Hawthorns on January 24, 1931. The Baggies edged Portsmouth and Wolves out by the odd goal in the next two rounds.

Glidden again to the fore as he heads home the only goal of Albion's FA Cup semi-final clash with Everton at Old Trafford. His winner, celebrated joyously by Albion fans in a crowd of 69,241, put the club through to their first Final at the twin towers. It was a bizarre long-range goal, watched here by W. G. Richardson.

The Everton v Albion semi-final did not pass without problems. The huge turn-out prompted thousands of fans to flee on to the pitch to escape the crush and there were casualties as mounted police ensured order was kept. Interest was increased because hosts Manchester United had a dismal Cup record at the time and were relegated from the First Division in this 1930-31 campaign.

Full throttle behind the scenes. Secretary Fred Everiss (left) and his assistant Eph Smith sift through the mammoth mail-bag filled by Albion fans hopefully seeking tickets for the club's FA Cup Final against Birmingham at Wembley in the spring of 1931. At the time, Albion were a Second Division club, although they were steaming towards promotion as well.

The next train to arrive at platform 1 …Albion's dapper players wait to board before going off to do battle with Blues at Wembley. No match-day tracksuits or mobile phones in those days! Left to right: J. S. Round (director), Tommy Glidden, Bert Trentham, W. G. Richardson, Harold Pearson, Bill Richardson, Tommy Magee (front), Teddy Sandford, Jimmy Edwards, Stan Wood, Jimmy Cookson, Bob Finch, Harry Boston, Fred Everiss (secretary-manager), W. I. Bassett (chairman), Fred Reed (trainer).

Into the cauldron. Fred Everiss leads Albion's expectant players, headed by skipper Tommy Glidden, into the Wembley spotlight for their all-Midlands Final against Birmingham. The crowd was 90,368.

Albion left-half Jimmy Edwards is greeted by the Duke of Gloucester before kick-off.

Birmingham and England 'keeper Harry Hibbs punches clear from Teddy Sandford.

Agony for Albion as centre-forward W. G. Richardson sees his header elude 'keeper Hibbs, drop on to the bar and then over. Richardson scored twice in the game – his 21st and 22nd goals of a season he entered only in November. This Billy Richardson was given the name 'W. G.' to distinguish himself from centre-half Bill Richardson, who was no relation but played in the same game and many others!

In goes No 1! W. G. Richardson watches the ball go into the Birmingham net for his and Albion's first goal in the 25th minute.

Winner on the way! Hibbs is left floundering as Richardson prepares to apply the killer touch almost immediately after Joe Bradford's equaliser for First Division Birmingham mid-way through the second half.

Well done lads! Skipper Tommy Glidden, the outside-right or inside-right who scored 140 goals in 479 competitive matches for the club, leads the victorious Albion players down Wembley's famous steps following their 2-1 triumph – the third time they had lifted the Cup.

The silverware returns to West Bromwich. Around 150,000 well-wishers greeted Albion's players back home – an emotional occasion during which there was this quieter moment for players (from left) Sandford, Magee, Trentham, Bill Richardson, W. G. Richardson, Carter, Wood and Shaw. They are joined by chairman Billy Bassett, directors J. S. Round and James Everiss and the Lord Mayor of West Bromwich.

Open-top bus ride 1931 style! Tommy Glidden shows off the FA Cup to the cheering masses.

Bert Trentham, Joe Carter, Tommy Glidden, Harold Pearson (behind), Teddy Sandford, Tommy Magee, Jimmy Edwards, W. G. Richardson and the FA Cup are the centre of attention among ecstatic admirers.

Although the FA Cup was safely under lock and key, Albion still had a little unfinished business in the League. They went into the final game of their historic 1930-31 season a week later on Saturday, May 2, knowing they had to beat visiting Charlton to be sure of returning to the First Division. And this they did, but only after a tremendous battle with the club who had taken the Baggies to three matches at the start of the Cup run. Charlton twice led in front of a then record Hawthorns gate of 52,415 but Teddy Sandford and Tommy Glidden came up with equalisers, then W. G. Richardson scored this fine headed winner in the 68th minute to set the scene for fantastic post-match scenes of celebration.

Albion's unique feat of winning the FA Cup and promotion in the same season – and no team have managed it since – prompted a visit by royalty. The Prince of Wales, later King Edward V111, was at The Hawthorns adding his congratulations on May 11, 1931, a plaque to commemorate his visit being proudly unveiled. Albion finished runners-up to Everton, seven points adrift, in the Second Division but, more importantly, were three ahead of third-placed Tottenham.

Back in the top flight with a win. Albion's four-year exile in the Second Division was ended in style with a 1-0 opening-day win against mighty Arsenal at Highbury on August 29, 1931. Here, George Shaw tries to cover a shot from the prolific Cliff Bastin, Arsenal's long-time record scorer before Ian Wright.

Albion's 5-1 First Division win against West Ham United at Upton Park on November 7, 1931. By the ninth minute, W. G. Richardson had scored four times in five minutes – one of the most astonishing sequences in English football history. Here, the Hammers are on the attack for once in the game as their centre-forward Vic Watson moves between Albion 'keeper Harold Pearson and full-back Bert Trentham. Teddy Sandford scored the Baggies' other goal in their fourth away win of the season.

Black Country derby-day images in the early 1930s. *Above*: Albion 'keeper Harold Pearson takes possession at The Hawthorns *Below*: It's Pearson again, this time denying Wolves star forward Billy Hartill at Molineux.

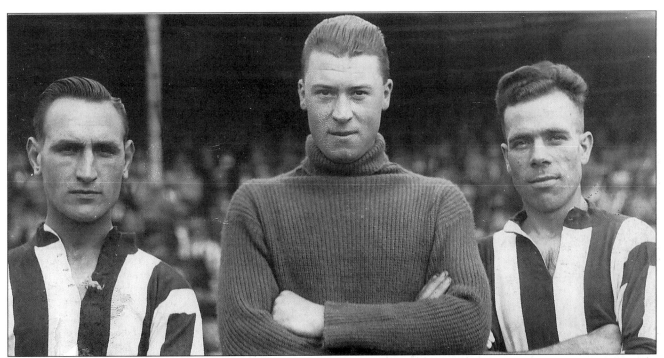

A 1932 picture of a formidable Albion defensive trio – from left, Bob Finch, Harold Pearson and George Shaw. Full-back Shaw, who picked up one England cap, made 425 senior appearances for the club. Pearson followed his father Hubert into Albion's goal and played 303 senior games for the club and, like Shaw, turned out in a solitary England match. Finch, a full-back, featured in 234 League and Cup games for the Baggies, his 14 years' loyal service also including the winning of three Central League titles with the reserve team he often skippered.

Pounding the Hawthorns beat in training are (from left) Billy Tudor, Dougie Witcomb, Billy Elliott and Jimmy Adams. Elliott, an outside-right who was a worthy but little-used challenger to Stanley Matthews' England shirt, scored in 11 successive games in 1941-42 – an Albion record. Keeper Adams was one of the club's heaviest players, making his debut in 1929 but playing most of his career during the Second World War. Witcomb made 122 Albion appearances and Tudor the more modest figure of 34.

Christmas Day football used to be big business, with local derbies the 'norm.' Here, on December 25, 1931, Albion's Joe Carter looks on as Birmingham 'keeper Harry Hibbs touches the ball to safety. Blues won this Hawthorns clash 1-0, repeated the victory at St Andrew's the following day and so gained some revenge for their Wembley defeat against the Baggies earlier in the year.

On the warpath again! W. G. Richardson closes in but Chelsea 'keeper Vic Woodley has things under control during one of Albion's two visits to Stamford Bridge in 1933-34. Albion lost 3-2 in the League in March, having drawn 1-1 in the third round of the Cup, only to go out after extra-time in the replay.

In February, 1935 The Hawthorns hosted an international trial game between England and The Rest. Here, the Arsenal centre-forward Ted Drake scores his second goal for the England team. A crowd of 12,845 saw the sides draw 2-2.

Action from Albion's 7-1 slamming of visiting Sheffield United in the fourth round of the 1934-35 FA Cup as 'keeper Harold Pearson takes control. The Baggies marched on to Wembley, where they were to meet the other Sheffield side, Wednesday.

The 1935 FA Cup Final prompted a change of colours for Albion and Sheffield Wednesday, the Baggies lining up in royal blue and white on the day and for this pre-Wembley picture. Back row, from left: F. Reed (trainer), W. H. Keys (director), H. Trentham, H. Pearson, J. Carter, J. Round (director), C. Jephcott (director). Middle row: L. Nurse (director), W. Richardson, W. G. Richardson, W. Bassett (chairman), T. Glidden, E. Sandford, F. Everiss (secretary). Front row: A. Gale, J. Edwards, G. Shaw, J. Murphy, W. Boyes, J. Sankey.

The Prince of Wales exchanges a friendly pre-match word with Fred Everiss, who doubled up as secretary and manager for many years. Skipper Tommy Glidden (left) made the introductions.

Spinning the coin are Albion captain Glidden and his Wednesday counterpart Ronnie Starling, watched by referee Mr A. E. Fogg.

Wednesday's goalkeeper Jack Brown, perhaps fearful of a then-legitimate shoulder charge, prepares to punch clear as a team-mate takes a tumble. Sheffield-born Wally Boyes, an England international, scored along with Ted Sandford for Albion, but Wednesday held the aces in a 4-2 victory.

Back to the drawing board. Albion players assemble for training at The Hawthorns in 1935. There was certainly no shortage of goals in 1935-36, the Baggies conceding 88 but scoring 89, including seven in a derby away win that helped condemn their victims Villa to relegation for the first time.

Pre-season training in 1936 at The Hawthorns. A few months later, the club were in mourning at the death of chairman Billy Bassett, whose astonishing 51-year association with Albion included sterling service as a right-winger. He won 16 England caps and played in three FA Cup Finals – in 1888, 1892 and 1895.

W. G. Richardson and Teddy Sandford stand by waiting for slips as Birmingham's defence come under pressure in Albion's first victory of the 1936-37 season. The Baggies had lost their opening match at home to Derby but bounced back to beat Blues 3-2.

Heading for the big drop. Albion are looking gloomily down the barrel as Don Dearson – later to guest for them in wartime football – fires home for Birmingham in the First Division clash at St Andrew's on Good Friday, 1938. Blues won 2-1 and Albion, who had heavily lost an FA Cup semi-final to Preston at Highbury the year before, were a few matches away from relegation. The following day, they lost 7-1 at Manchester City and there was to be no escape.

Down – and Up Again!

Albion embarked on their second season as a Division Two club in 1946-47 when football resumed in its recognised form following the war. In the meantime, the FA Cup was staged in 1946 and Albion recorded a notable third-round scalp in a campaign in which the competition was played, unusually, over two legs. They hammered top-flight Cardiff 4-0 at The Hawthorns after this 1-1 draw at Ninian Park.

Foiled again. Sam Bartram was in imperious form when Charlton visited a snow-hit Black Country in the fourth round of the FA Cup on January 25, 1947. Here, he takes a routine high ball as the Londoners won 2-1 in the year they won the competition.

Stars, too, at the snooker table! Billy Elliott prepares to pot, watched by (left to right) Jim Pemberton, Tommy Grimley (with pipe), George Drury, Harry Kinsell, Len Millard, Cliff Edwards and Cecil Shaw, in an off-beat scene from during the 1946-47 season.

Albion players check in at The Hawthorns on a summer's morning in August, 1947. They are (left to right): Aldridge, Hood, Richards, Elliott, W. G. Richardson (assistant trainer), Tighe, Walsh, Kinsell, Hodgetts, Pemberton.

Get in! George Drury (No 8) scores one of his two goals in Albion's 3-2 Second Division win over Brentford at The Hawthorns on September 20, 1947. It was the club's sixth victory in nine games in a promising start to the campaign, particularly for Drury. But they fell away and had to spend another season in Division Two.

Frank Hodgetts is foiled by Brentford 'keeper Joe Crozier in the same game during a season which was to prove a watershed. In 1948, Fred Everiss resigned after 46 years as secretary – and the club had more than 100 applications to take over a role which also included that of manager.

Pleased to see you again! Jack Vernon, one of Albion's finest centre-halves after being bought for the club from Belfast Celtic for a then club record £9,500, greets his West Ham counterpart Sam Small before the Baggies' 2-1 home League defeat on October 25, 1947. Vernon was to play exactly 200 games for Albion as well as winning 22 full caps for his country, captaining the United Kingdom side and playing for Great Britain against the Rest of the World.

Keeper Jim Sanders rushes out to challenge Tottenham's Peter Murphy during the 3-1 FA Cup fourth-round defeat at White Hart Lane in 1947-48. Reg 'Paddy' Ryan looks on.

On the way to promotion. Centre-forward Dave Walsh, holder of 11 Northern Ireland caps and 20 for the Republic, heads one of the 23 League goals in 1948-49 with which he helped Albion back to the First Division. This effort came in a 2-0 February 5 win against Brentford at The Hawthorns as the Baggies powered on in the first season in which they had a full-time manager. The first man to fill the post was Jack Smith, a former trialist and wartime player for the club.

The ball is just a blur in the foreground as Dave Walsh finds his scoring boots again. This time, it's Fulham on the receiving end, despite an unsporting shout by a defender, as a right-foot shot helps Albion to a 4-1 win in December, 1949, in their first season back in Division One.

Back in the Top Flight

Jim Sanders is beaten as Len Duquemin heads the second of Tottenham's five goals in a 5-0 mauling of Albion at White Hart Lane in March, 1951. Duquemin went on to complete his hat-trick and Tottenham, who had only just ended a 15-year exile in the Second Division, became League champions in their first season back in the top flight.

He flies through the air …the legendary Nat Lofthouse launches himself full length to direct a header at Albion's goal in a third-round FA Cup tie in January, 1952. He was out of luck, though, and the Baggies, having traded 3-2 wins with the Trotters on Christmas Day and Boxing Day, ran out 4-0 victors.

The end of the dream for another year. After beating Gateshead 2-0 at Newcastle in round four, Albion reached the end of the FA Cup road with this fifth-round 1-0 defeat at Blackburn. Referee Arthur Ellis has just awarded the home side a penalty for hand-ball against white-shirted left-back Len Millard.

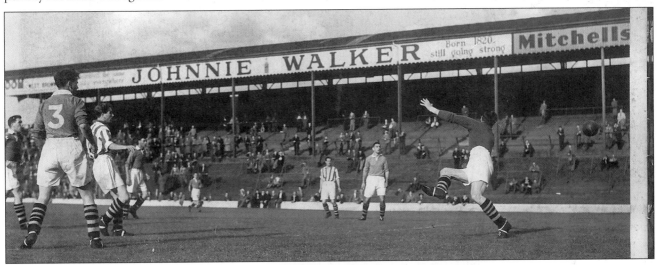

Another feature of yesteryear – the full-scale pre-season trial game. In this version in the summer of 1952, Jim Sanders does well to tip round the post from the stripe-shirted Johnny Nicholls. The Wolverhampton-born goal-poacher had made his senior debut a few months earlier.

Ouch! Albion forward Evans collides with the Stoke goalkeeper in the home side's 3-2 Division One win at The Hawthorns in September, 1952. The ball went into the net but the goal was disallowed.

Action from Albion's 1-1 League draw with Wolves in the autumn of 1952. *Above*: Norman Heath deals safely with a high ball under pressure from Roy Swinbourne as Joe Kennedy and Dennis Wilshaw stand by. *Below:* It's Wolves 'keeper Nigel Sims' turn to come under threat as he opts to punch away with Ronnie Allen challenging.

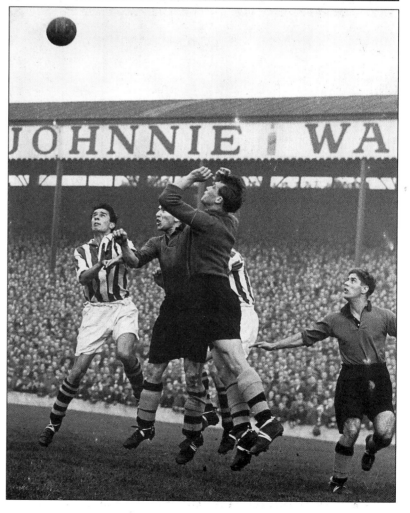

Liverpool tamed! The Merseysiders survive this attack on their area but a goal by Ronnie Allen (left) and two from Frank Griffin saw Albion to maximum points early in the 1952-53 programme. It was the Baggies' fifth successive League victory.

Not quite! Johnny Nicholls can't twist enough to head home on Albion's trip to Derby in November, 1952. George Lee did find the target, though, and the Baggies collected a 1-1 draw at the Baseball Ground.

An unusual wide-angled shot of Albion players at work away from the gaze of the masses in 1952 – the year Jack Smith passed

Anxiety in the Wolves goalmouth as left-winger George Lee heads Albion's equaliser three minutes from the end of the Black Country draw

the managerial reins over to Jesse Carver, who lasted only eight months in the post.

at The Hawthorns on October 18, 1952. The goal came from a cross by Frank Griffin (far right), with Evans, Allen and Ryan up in support.

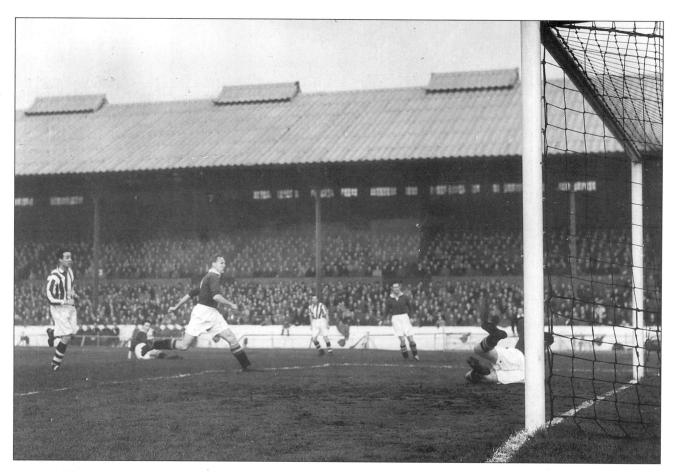

Albion and Chelsea became highly familiar with each other in 1952-53. Each won at the other's ground in the First Division while their FA Cup fourth-round meeting went to no fewer than four games. Eventually, Chelsea won a third replay at Highbury 4-0 – Albion's last defeat in the competition for two years. In these pictures from the League clash at Stamford Bridge, Ronnie Allen scores to put his side on the way to a 2-0 win (above) while (right) Jimmy Dudley is the in-danger meat in the sandwich as his 'keeper Norman Heath punches away from Chelsea's Les Stubbs.

Slip-slide time at The Hawthorns. Manchester United's Cockburn fails to connect with a McShane corner as Albion defend in depth on their way to a 3-1 League win in the snow on November 29, 1952.

The weather was so grim that only 23,617 turned up for the visit of League champions United. Matt Busby's side were put firmly in the shade for the day, although Eddie Lewis beat the diving Norman Heath here to score their consolation goal.

Debut day for Jimmy Dugdale and the defender does well here to harass England centre-forward Nat Lofthouse in Albion's 1-0 defeat at home to Bolton in December, 1952. Dugdale was deputising for Joe Kennedy and went on to receive FA Cup winners' medals with both Albion and Villa.

Albion were a major First Division force in 1952-53 and proved too good on this occasion for the Preston side they were to meet again in more famous surroundings just over a year later. Ronnie Allen and North End centre-half Marston are captured here in combat but it was Johnny Nicholls and Paddy Ryan who scored in Albion's 2-1 New Year win.

Start of a long-running FA Cup saga. Albion's defence survive a Chelsea corner in their FA Cup fourth-round tie at Stamford Bridge on January 31, 1953. The sides drew 1-1 and were then deadlocked 0-0 after extra-time at The Hawthorns and 1-1 over 120 minutes in a second replay at Villa Park. Bizarrely, Chelsea romped home 4-0 in the fourth clash, at Highbury.

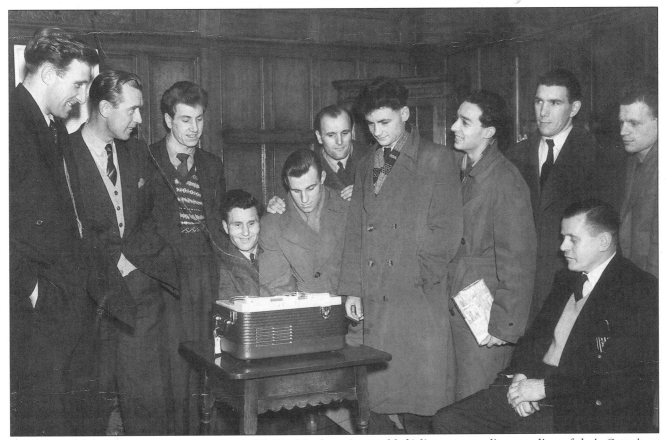

On the air. Albion players and new manager Vic Buckingham (second left) listen to a radio recording of their Cup tie at Chelsea.

Arsenal's Cliff Holton has just scored in the 2-2 draw at Highbury on 21 March, 1953 as West Brom take a point off that season's eventual League champions. The Albion players (left to right) are Jimmy Dugdale (5), Len Millard (3), goalkeeper Norman Heath and right-back Stan Rickaby on the goal-line.

A brave header by Ronnie Allen gives Albion one of the goals which beat Manchester City 2-1 in the League game at The Hawthorns on February 7, 1953. It was one of Allen's 234 goals for the club – a record that stood until Tony Brown left it 'for dead' in the 1970s.

Cup KO. Albion and 'keeper Norman Heath survive this shot by the dark-shirted Roy Bentley but Chelsea scored four to finally resolve their four-game epic in this third replay at Highbury.

Safely over. A shot from Wilf Mannion flies high of the target as Jimmy Dugdale, Ray Barlow, Stan Rickaby and 'keeper Norman Heath close ranks in Albion's 3-0 home win over Middlesbrough in February, 1953. The goals came from Allen (2) and Lee.

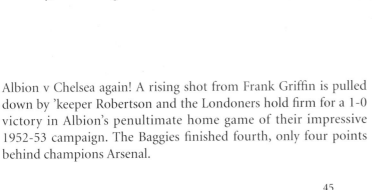

Albion v Chelsea again! A rising shot from Frank Griffin is pulled down by 'keeper Robertson and the Londoners hold firm for a 1-0 victory in Albion's penultimate home game of their impressive 1952-53 campaign. The Baggies finished fourth, only four points behind champions Arsenal.

The masterful goal-poacher! Johnny Nicholls adds the finishing touch to a Frank Griffin cross and puts Albion on the way to a 2-1 win at home to Middlesbrough on October 3, 1953. It was to prove Albion's finest-ever season.

One week on and Huddersfield are put to the sword. Ronnie Allen is thwarted here by 'keeper Mills as Paddy Ryan hopes to pick up the pieces. But Allen scored a hat-trick and Nicholls also found the net as Albion cruised home 4-0.

So Near to the Double

HAVING created football history in 1930-31 by becoming the first club to win the FA Cup and promotion from the Second Division in the same season, Albion went close to an even more glorious landmark 23 seasons later.

The League and Cup double was theirs for the taking – until it was heartbreakingly snatched away from them by, of all teams, Wolves!

While progressing towards Wembley thanks to wins over Chelsea, Rotherham, Newcastle and Tottenham, Albion were also strongly in contention for the championship.

By the turn of the year, Huddersfield had virtually dropped out of a three-cornered fight for the title that also embraced the men from Molineux. And, when Vic Buckingham's side edged unconvincingly past Port Vale – who were chasing promotion from the Third Division North – in the Cup semi-final at Villa Park on March 27, the double was very much on.

On the same day, Wolves had lost 4-2 at home to Middlesbrough, so Albion led the race by two points. But the First Division run-in at The Hawthorns was to be plagued by great misfortune.

At Sunderland on the last day of the month, the Baggies' Wolverhampton-born goalkeeper Norman Heath collided with Sunderland's former Birmingham forward Ted Purdon and was carried off on a stretcher. The popular Heath was found to have a serious neck injury that was to prevent him playing again.

Ray Barlow went in goal for most of the game and played brilliantly, but couldn't prevent Albion – playing the midweek match in the daytime because Roker Park had no floodlights – slipping to a costly 2-1 defeat.

Even so, as Jim Sanders – a former bomber pilot who was injured in the war – prepared to take over in goal, the omens were good for the Baggies. Going into the start of April, they led their near neighbours by two points, both clubs having six League matches to play.

Intriguingly, one of those games was between the two of them at The Hawthorns on April 3, when outside 'interference' had an influence that was astonishing by today's standards.

On the same day, England were playing Scotland at Hampden Park, so out of the Black Country clash at the demands of the international selectors went four players. Billy Wright and Jimmy Mullen were huge stars of Stan Cullis's Wolves line-up but maybe Albion were harder hit by the two withdrawals they suffered – forwards Ronnie Allen and Johnny Nicholls, who had scored around two-thirds of their side's goals between them during the season.

The result was a 1-0 win for Wolves, who had not triumphed at the ground in the League since 1928. Roy Swinbourne's hooked winner also meant the Wanderers had become the first club to do the double over Albion in 1953-54. Consequently, Wolves led the table on their infinitely superior goal-average and the tide had turned.

Buckingham had been able to field only five of his regular 11 against Wolves and, when Stuart Williams and Paddy Ryan became limping passengers during the following Saturday's game at Cardiff, he must have thought the club's luck was out.

Albion had plenty of the play but lost 2-0 in front of a Ninian Park crowd of more than 50,000 while Wolves made no such mistakes as they demolished Charlton 5-0 at Molineux to go two points clear with four games remaining.

Next time out, the scales tilted partially back in Albion's favour as victory at home to Manchester City on Easter Saturday – secured by a Ronnie Allen penalty – coincided with Wolves' 0-0 draw at Sheffield Wednesday.

But Wolves took a major grip in the matches that followed on the Monday and Tuesday of the holiday programme. They sent Huddersfield packing from Molineux and could even afford to slip 2-1 to the same opponents the following day because Albion had an unrewarding time in their double-header against Aston Villa.

Nicholls's breakthrough goal at The Hawthorns was followed by a Peter McParland equaliser in a 1-1 draw, then Villa ran riot the following day with five goals in the first 35 minutes. Frank Griffin pulled one back but a Barlow own-goal put the seal on a sad 6-1 hammering for Albion, and the title was as good as draped in old gold and black.

It would have taken a freak combination of last-day results for Albion to overhaul their rivals as the Baggies went to Portsmouth while Wolves squared up to visiting Tottenham. There were no such further twists.

Wolves saw Spurs off 2-0 and Albion, with one eye on their Cup Final clash with Preston a week later, slipped up 3-0 at Fratton Park. Wolves were champions for the first time in the Football League's 66-year history – by a final margin of four points – and Albion made it a magnificent year for the West Midlands by winning 3-2 at Wembley. But it was the season Albion could easily have become the first club this century to do the League and Cup double.

A key game in what was to prove a thrilling title race. Wolves and England 'keeper Bert Williams goes down to save a point-blank shot from George Lee in Albion's 1-0 defeat at Molineux on November 14.

Wembley here we come! In front of more than 61,000 crammed into The Hawthorns, Albion turned on the style to beat Newcastle 3-2 in an FA Cup fifth-round tie that lived long in the minds of those who saw it. An estimated 20,000 were locked out as Albion, playing in red shirts and white shorts, edged through thanks to a brilliant hat-trick by Allen, who is denied here by a diving save from Ronnie Simpson.

This time Simpson grabs the ball after the Newcastle defence allowed Johnny Nicholls to break free. The Albion forward shot for goal, only to see Simpson dive to his left to smother the effort.

Albion on the attack in the Cup semi-final at Villa Park. Third Division North Port Vale resisted bravely in front of a 68,221 attendance but were finally sunk by a penalty from one of their former players, Ronnie Allen. In this attack, Allen and Johnny Nicholls harrass centre-half Cheadle as Jimmy Dudley's right-wing cross bounced in luckily for Albion's equaliser.

Back to the League – another nail in the coffin. Cardiff 2 Albion 0. Bill Baker eludes Albion's defenders to get in a shot.

The thin claret and blue wall! Ronnie Allen's explosive free-kick exposes a few gaps in Villa's rearguard in the 1-1 Easter Monday draw at The Hawthorns. The following day, inspired Villa won the re-match 6-1 and Albion as good as conceded the title to Wolves and had to settle for runners-up spot.

Wembley countdown. Albion directors in conference prior to the FA Cup Final against Preston. Chairman Mr H. Wilson Keys is in the centre and manager Vic Buckingham – in his first full season and destined to stay for five more – on the far left.

Wembley 'probables.' Albion line up shortly before their big day. Back row (from left): Joe Kennedy, Stuart Williams, Jimmy Dudley, Jim Sanders, Arthur Fitton (trainer), Ray Barlow, Jimmy Dugdale, Len Millard. Front: Frank Griffin, Paddy Ryan, Ronnie Allen, Johnny Nicholls, George Lee. The unlucky player come selection-time was defender Stuart Williams.

Messing about on the river. Albion players take to the Thames from their pre-Wembley hideaway near Reading to unwind before the big game. On their way to the twin towers, Albion had enjoyed the luck of the draw, beating Chelsea (H) 1-0, Rotherham (H) 4-0, Newcastle (H) 3-2 and Tottenham (H) 3-0 as well as Port Vale (at Villa Park) 2-1.

Ronnie Allen is captured in respectful pose as he is introduced to the Queen Mother. Nearest the camera is 'keeper Jim Sanders, in the side because first-choice Norman Heath had suffered a serious career-ending neck injury in a League game at Sunderland a month earlier.

Allen strikes to put Albion ahead, touching George Lee's cross into an unguarded net.

Goal for Preston as Angus Morrison heads home despite the attentions of Joe Kennedy. This 22nd minute equaliser came 60 seconds after Allen's opener.

Jim Sanders saves bravely at the feet of Charlie Wayman, who put Preston ahead early in the second half with a goal Albion claimed was offside.

One of the most famous pictures in Cup Final history. Penalty king Ronnie Allen keeps his nerve to drive home Albion's equaliser at 2-2 – much to the relief of half of the 99,852 crowd. Frank Griffin fired in the winner three minutes from time.

Despair in Preston's goalmouth after Frank Griffin scores the winning goal to give Albion the Cup.

FA Cup winners for the fourth time! Skipper Len Millard is chaired by jubilant team-mates (from left) Ray Barlow, Jimmy Dugdale, Paddy Ryan, Jim Sanders, Frank Griffin and Ronnie Allen.

Match-winner Griffin, accompanied by Barlow and two-goal Allen, kisses the boot responsible for the late Wembley decider – the right-winger's seventh and most important goal of the season. Griffin went on to make 275 senior appearances for the club, scoring 52 goals.

A stroll in Hyde Park for the winners! George Lee, Paddy Ryan, Jimmy Dudley and Ray Barlow take a celebratory walkabout before heading back to the Midlands from London.

Top right: Time for home. Albion players prepare to board their train at Paddington Station, accompanied by an item of valuable cargo – the FA Cup.

Bottom right: The financial spoils of success. From the competition organisers, a cheque for £6,894.15s 10d.

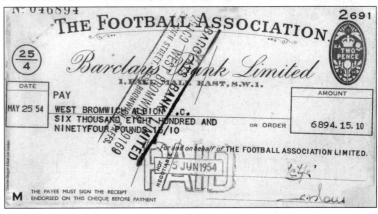

Lest we forget. Stan Rickaby (centre) and Norman Heath (right) both had the misfortune of missing the FA Cup Final, so Lord Dartmouth (left) presented them with replica winners' medals at a club dinner at The Hawthorns in July, 1954. The duo suffered injuries several weeks earlier. Rickaby duly returned the following season but 'keeper Heath, who seriously hurt his neck, would never add to his 169 senior games for the club.

There or Thereabouts

England manager-to-be Alf Ramsey keeps guard alongside Johnny Nicholls at the far post as Tottenham 'keeper Ted Ditchburn fails to gather a ball from Frank Griffin in Albion's 3-1 defeat at White Hart Lane on October 9, 1954 – a game that followed a run of seven wins in nine matches.

Charlton are the opposition in this snow-hit League clash at The Valley in 1956. Don Howe prepares to bring the ball out of danger, with Len Millard and Jim Sanders in close attendance.

At full stretch. George Lee, who made close to 300 Albion appearances and scored 65 goals, extends himself but can't quite get to the ball ahead of Burnley 'keeper Colin McDonald in a 2-2 League draw at The Hawthorns in September, 1956.

In 1956-57, Albion once again had the scent of Wembley in their nostrils. Having beaten Doncaster in a replay and Sunderland, they found themselves up against Blackpool in round five. Jimmy Dudley (left) and Don Howe come to the support of 'keeper Jim Sanders in a 0-0 draw at Bloomfield Road.

There wasn't much in it back at The Hawthorns either but Albion edged through with this 2-1 replay success. Here, Blackpool 'keeper George Farm saves well from Ronnie Allen, who nevertheless made the score-sheet, along with Derek Kevan.

Arsenal were next on Albion's Cup agenda and, in an exciting Hawthorns quarter-final, Gunners full-back Len Wills clears as 'keeper Jack Kelsey goes down and Brian Whitehouse hovers.

The Albion-Arsenal tie ended 2-2 in front of 53,459 fans, with 'keeper Sanders taking control of this situation as No 2 Don Howe (later to play, coach and manage at Highbury), Ray Barlow, Joe Kennedy and Jimmy Dudley are joined by the Gunners' Derek Tapscott and Cliff Holton.

A happy Highbury replay. Brian Whitehouse fires in one of Albion's goals in their 2-1 win at Arsenal on March 5, 1957. The success put Vic Buckingham's side through to face Villa in the semi-final.

Molineux was the setting for the clash of the two West Midlands rivals during a remarkable Midlands-dominated semi-final weekend in which Birmingham were meeting Manchester United at Hillsborough. Brian Whitehouse was again to the fore, scoring twice, one of his goals captured here before Villa equalised at 2-2 with five minutes left.

Blues, having gone out to United, had the consolation of staging the Albion v Villa replay. Albion lost the injured Ronnie Allen inside the first 20 minutes, conceded the only goal of the game to Billy Myerscough and then tried valiantly for a way back. A lunging Brian Whitehouse is beaten here by 'keeper Nigel Sims as Pat Saward covers. A total of more than 113,000 fans watched the games at Molineux and St Andrew's.

Off to see the mysteries of Russia. Albion players congregate at Snow Hill Station for the first leg of their three-match tour in the summer of 1957. Pictured are (back row, from left): Ray Barlow, Stuart Williams, Ronnie Allen, Joe Kennedy, Maurice Setters, George Lee, Jim Sanders, Fred Brown, Jimmy Dudley, Frank Griffin, Len Millard, Bobby Robson. Front: Ray Horobin, Brian Whitehouse. Don Howe and Derek Kevan also linked up with the squad.

Proud moment. Ray Barlow leads Albion out to face Zenit Leningrad in the first of the club's three matches against top-flight opposition on Russian soil. 'Greetings to the Sportsmen of Great Britain' says the sign above the tunnel.

Joe Kennedy puts his head in the way of a Zenit cross as 'keeper Fred Brown waits to collect. On the right is Don Howe. A goal by Derek Kevan earned a 1-1 draw for Albion, who went on to beat Dinamo Tbilisi 3-1 thanks to goals by Kevan (2) and Horobin, then overpower a Russian Army side 4-2 with Kevan (2), Allen and Horobin on the mark.

A joyous leap from Bobby Robson as he scores one of his two goals in the 2-0 First Division win at Nottingham Forest on September 28, 1957. The week before, Albion had crushed Manchester 9-2 at The Hawthorns, with Frank Griffin scoring a hat-trick.

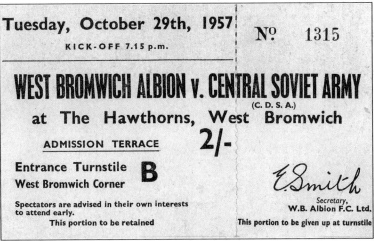

Tuesday, October 29th, 1957
KICK-OFF 7.15 p.m.

Nº 1315

WEST BROMWICH ALBION v. CENTRAL SOVIET ARMY
(C. D. S. A.)
at The Hawthorns, West Bromwich

ADMISSION TERRACE 2/-

Entrance Turnstile **B**
West Bromwich Corner

Spectators are advised in their own interests to attend early.

This portion to be retained

E.Smith
Secretary,
W.B. Albion F.C. Ltd.

This portion to be given up at turnstile

A rare collector's item …a two shilling ticket from the night at the start of Albion's floodlit era when they took on the visiting Central Soviet Army side in a friendly in October, 1957. The game, arranged to mark the opening of the club's £18,000 lights, brought the Baggies a 6-5 victory.

Bobby Robson, later to manage England in more than 90 games, played 257 matches (61 goals) for Albion in between two spells at Fulham. A right-half converted from an inside-right, he also played 20 times for his country. Here, he challenges Sunderland's 'keeper Fraser at The Hawthorns in the home's side 3-0 win in November, 1957 – a game in which he scored.

Sadness hung thick in the air when Albion went to Old Trafford for an FA Cup quarter-final replay in March, 1958. Only a month earlier, Manchester United had lost eight of their players in the Munich Disaster – and Black Country boy Duncan Edwards was later to die from his injuries. United, on a wave of emotion, somehow found it in themselves to reach the Cup Final that season, helped by this last-minute winner from Colin Webster against Albion, who, three days later, won 4-0 in the League at the same ground.

Derek Kevan swoops for one of his 173 Albion goals – from only 291 appearances. This one set up a 4-0 win against visiting Everton on March 15, 1958. The Yorkshire-born centre-forward, who won 14 England caps, had the Merseysiders on the rack in a massive way when he scored five against them in a 6-2 victory just over a year later.

Moment of impact. Roy Horobin seems to have knocked the ball out of shape as he crosses on the run in the First Division home defeat against Wolves on March 29, 1958.

End of a gloomy six-game League run. Albion had lost four and drawn two before they found their scoring boots in this 6-2 romp against Leicester in their penultimate home match of 1957-58. Brian Whitehouse, later a member of the club's backroom staff, scored twice (one of which is pictured above). Albion No 8 Bobby Robson had an even better day, hitting a hat-trick (one of which is pictured below) and pushing himself towards a final goal tally of 27 for the campaign.

A young Graham Williams looks on as Clive Jackman dives to push the ball away from Arsenal's Jimmy Bloomfield during Albion's 4-3 First Division defeat at Highbury in October, 1958. The 'keeper was playing the last-but-one of his 21 League matches for the club.

In the same clash with the Gunners, Derek Kevan scored a hat-trick. Here, he falls as one of his three goals whistles in.

With their Cup hopes ended at Blackpool in round five, Albion returned to League action to seal a final placing of fifth despite this 3-1 defeat at West Ham in early March. Ray Potter dives but can't stop Malcolm Musgrove scoring, watched by Joe Kennedy. When Albion faced another side in claret and blue, Villa, on the last day of the season, there was an extraordinary twist. Ronnie Allen equalised two minutes from time to send Villa down.

Safe hands. Albion 'keeper Ray Potter hangs on safely to this cross despite an aerial challenge from Peter Dobing in a goalless First Division draw at Ewood Park on April 4, 1959.

Don't worry, I'll come home safe! Albion left-half Ray Barlow gives daughter Lesley a loving kiss before departing on the club's six-week tour of Canada and the USA in the summer of 1959. The Baggies scored 59 goals in their nine matches, losing only once. Barlow, unlucky to win only one England cap, played 482 games for Albion, scoring 48 goals and captaining them in the late 1950s.

There's something moving in the long grass! Albion players limber up for the 1959-60 before the groundsman gave the pitch a good cut. The squad reported back under a new manager, Gordon Clark having taken over from Vic Buckingham, who quit to coach Ajax.

New season, same old menace. Derek Kevan lunges in but can't get the touch to beat Tottenham 'keeper Bill Brown in Albion's first defeat of 1959-60 – 2-1 at The Hawthorns in the club's fourth game.

Down goes Derek Kevan and it's a penalty for Albion in their comfortable 3-0 victory over visiting Leeds on September 19, 1959. Goals came from Ronnie Allen (2) and Bobby Robson.

Ouch, that one hurt! Bobby Robson receives attention from trainer Dick Graham and a St John's Ambulance man during Albion's 4-1 early-autumn defeat at West Ham. The wing-half missed only one game all season – and that in April.

Cup-time again and Bolton are ushered to a fourth-round exit by this 2-0 defeat at The Hawthorns. Dave Burnside, seen here challenging with Derek Kevan (right), scored one goal and Alec Jackson got the other.

Jock Wallace is caught out as Norman Deeley scores the second goal for defending League champions Wolves in their 3-1 First Division home win over Albion on February 27, 1960. Bobby Mason follows up just in case while Wolverhampton-born Don Howe is helpless in the background.

Goalkeeper Jock Wallace, later to become manager at Filbert Street, punches clear as Graham Williams lends his support during Albion's 2-1 FA Cup fifth-round defeat at Leicester on February 20, 1960. It was the fifth successive year in which Albion had reached at least the fifth round, only to go out before Wembley. And some lean Cup years were to follow before the good times returned in the mid-1960s.

If Albion were disappointed at Molineux, they were inspired at St Andrew's two months later on Good Friday, destroying Birmingham 7-1. *Above:* Ronnie Allen drives in one of the goals that made up his hat-trick while *(right)* the forward and team-mates Jock Wallace and three-goal Derek Kevan make their way through their admirers at the final whistle. The sides drew 1-1 at The Hawthorns the next day.

Midtable Respectability

Albion 'keeper Ray Potter gets his fingertips to a Wolves cross but can only knock it down for Norman Deeley to score in another West Midlands derby – this time at Molineux on January 28, 1961. Graham Williams and Bobby Robson are the other Baggies players in view.

Mid-table respectability was the extent of Albion's achievements in 1960-61, underlined by this 3-0 victory over visiting Everton. Alec Jackson is the scorer on this occasion, watched by young winger Clive Clark in the foreground.

Villa, having made an immediate return to Division One in 1960, were the Hawthorns visitors on October 21, 1961. Alec Jackson hurtles in here but is denied in the 1-1 draw by 'keeper Geoff Sidebottom, with John Sleeuwenhoek also on hand. It was Albion's first game under the managership of Scot Archie Macaulay.

1-1 was also the score when Albion welcomed FA Cup holders Wolves, this time on Boxing Day. *Above*: Bobby Robson, in his last season at The Hawthorns, winces as centre-half Stan Jones challenges Alan Hinton. *Below*: Jock Wallace dives bravely at the feet of Peter Broadbent and blocks as Jones and Robson close in.

A sweet triumph at Molineux. Five players are airborne in this piece of action from Albion's 2-1 FA Cup fourth-round win away to Wolves on January 27, 1962. Clive Clark scored both goals but the Baggies went out 4-2 at home to Tottenham in the next round.

Keith Smith, who scored 34 goals in only 70 first-team games at The Hawthorns, flies in at full stretch in Albion's 2-1 First Division win at Tottenham on April 21, 1962. Derek Kevan hit both goals against the side who had a few months earlier become the first to do the League and Cup double in England this century.

Striding out proudly. Albion and England right-back Don Howe prepares to receive the Midland Footballer of the Year award before the club's final game of 1961-62 – a 7-1 thumping of Blackpool. Howe included a spell as club captain in a 379-game Hawthorns career and also played 23 consecutive games for England. He returned to the club as manager in 1971.

Wintry scenes at Molineux on Boxing Day of 1962. Ray Potter is on his knees and the ball is in the back of his net for the second time, put there by Chris Crowe after Alan Hinton had fired Wolves ahead. Albion were mightily relieved when the game was abandoned at half-time – but their smiles turned to frowns when they lost 7-0 in the re-match!

Close call! Ray Potter dives, Stan Jones looks on anxiously and Arsenal's Geoff Strong waits to pick up the pieces in Albion's 3-2 First Division defeat at Highbury on Good Friday, 1963 – Jimmy Hagan's first game in charge.

Arsenal away on Good Friday, Blackburn away on Easter Saturday! Ray Potter dives in a vain attempt to stop Bryan Douglas's penalty in the Baggies' 3-1 defeat at Ewood Park on April 13. Bobby Hope, pictured hands on hips in the background, scored for the second day running.

Agony for Bobby Hope as he is helped off injured on the opening day of Albion's 1963-64 season at home to Leicester. The Scottish midfielder, signed four years earlier straight from school, played only three more League games all season – all in November.

In the same 1-1 draw, Albion right-back Bobby Cram, uncle of athlete Steve Cram, tangles with Leicester centre-half Ian King

Alec Jackson gives the grounded Geoff Strong the slip during Albion's 3-3 FA Cup fourth-round draw with Arsenal at The Hawthorns in January, 1964. Tipton-born Jackson scored 52 goals in 208 Baggies games.

Don Howe clears Albion's lines on this occasion but it was a temporary respite in their 2-0 FA Cup replay exit against Arsenal at Highbury. Doug Fraser and 'keeper Ray Potter patrol on the line.

Getting a kick. Doug Fraser gets to the ball first but not before receiving a painful blow from Sheffield United's Keith Kettleborough in Albion's 2-1 defeat at Bramall Lane in their final away game of 1963-64.

Jimmy Hagan was a stern disciplinarian in his time as Albion boss but his orders seem to be attracting approval in this pre-season shot from the summer of 1964. Forming the front row are (from left) Ian Collard, Bobby Hope, Doug Fraser, Ken Foggo, Ronnie Fenton and Tony Brown.

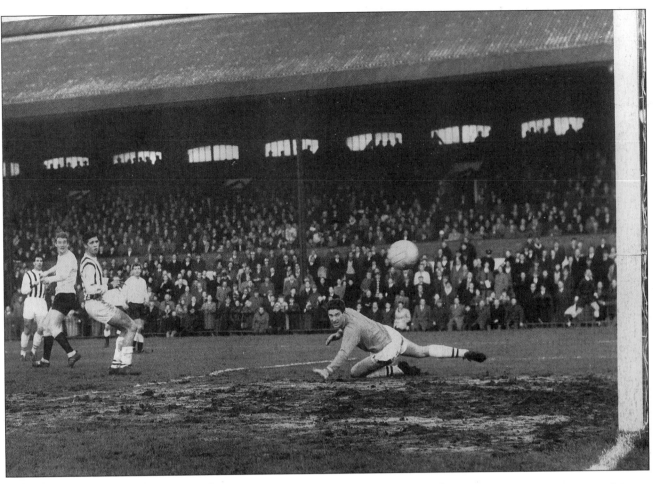

Knowing backward glances from Ray Fairfax, Graham Lovett and Ray Potter as Rodney Marsh blasts in one of the goals with which Fulham beat Albion 3-1 in the First Division at Craven Cottage just before Christmas, 1964. The crowd was only 10,390.

Melee near the line as Albion full-back Ray Fairfax holds off the attentions of Andy Lochhead in a 1-0 win over Burnley at Turf Moor on February 6, 1965.

No mistake! Bobby Cram had few equals in the art of taking penalties and was characteristically sure in driving home from the spot in this 3-1 derby win over Villa on February 27, 1965. Earlier in the season, right-back Cram, who totalled 26 goals from his 163 Albion games, scored a hat-trick in a 5-3 home win against Stoke, two of them penalties.

Some joy at last at Highbury! Despite George Eastham's goal after shrugging off Doug Fraser and Graham Williams (above), Albion took a point on their League visit to Arsenal on April 3, 1965. Bobby Hope scored for Jimmy Hagan's side, who survived this near-miss from Joe Baker, (right), with Williams again the covering defender.

Oh Dear! Although Stan Jones and Ray Potter repel this West Ham raid on Albion's goal on Good Friday, 1965, they had no answer to Hammers striker Brian Dear, who scored five times in 21 minutes starting just before half-time. The final score was 6-1.

Shell-shocked from their trip to Upton Park, Albion were in action in London again the following day when they took on Chelsea. And, despite this goal from Barry Bridges, floated in over centre-half Stan Jones and 'keeper Ray Potter, there was satisfaction to be had from a 2-2 draw secured by goals from Ray Crawford and Gerry Howshall.

A man called Jeff Astle had appeared on the Hawthorns scene early in 1964-65, signed from Notts County for only £25,000. He scored 11 goals in 33 games in what remained of his first season, then cut loose at the start of 1965-66. This header at home to Sheffield Wednesday helped him towards an autumn hat-trick – a feat he repeated within a week when his side won 4-3 on a Friday night at Northampton to go top of the First Division.

Swinging Sixties of Cup Successes

CUP success came in large helpings to West Bromwich Albion in the second half of the 1960s. In four years from the spring of 1966, a few weeks before English football's finest hour, they reached four major Cup Finals, lost in a semi-final and reached the last eight in the European Cup-winners' Cup.

And they did it largely with a settled side who grew up together as feared fighters in the knockout game; a group of players who made only a modest impact in the League but who had few equals in the sudden-death version.

Alan Ashman's side of 1968 FA Cup winners were very much seasoned professionals, taken from various corners of the UK. Graham Williams, Jeff Astle, John Osborne, John Talbut, Clive Clark and John Kaye had been signed from lesser clubs, Doug Fraser and Bobby Hope had arrived as youngsters from Scotland – a country later to send the likes of Asa Hartford, Ray Wilson, Jim Holton and Alistair Robertson down to The Hawthorns – while Tony Brown, Ian Collard and Birmingham boy Graham Lovett had joined the club straight from school.

Among those who played just before or just after the famous win over Everton, goalkeeper Ray Potter, Bobby Cram, Ken Foggo, Stan Jones and Len Cantello all had appearance tallies running well into three figures. Then came the 1970s and a new generation led by the likes of John Wile. Loyal men, indeed.

Team spirit was undoubtedly a key commodity in hauling the club through some extremely testing occasions in the heady late-1960s.

In a fourth-round FA Cup replay at Southampton in 1968, they lost John Osborne through concussion, the eccentric 'keeper being monitored from near his post for several minutes by trainer Stuart Williams before it was decided he could not carry on.

Left-back and skipper Graham Williams took over in goal and Albion dug deep into their considerable resolve to emerge with a 3-2 win in extra-time thanks to Astle's late strike.

The club, having luckily emerged with a replay from a third-round trip to Colchester – the minnows were crushed 4-0 at The Hawthorns – then defeated Portsmouth 2-1 at Fratton Park in round five before being drawn at home to mighty Liverpool at the quarter-final stage.

It was tight and tense in a goalless deadlock and few would then have given much for the chances of Ashman's side. They had lost 4-1 at Anfield in the League a few weeks earlier and gone down 2-0 to the same opponents at The Hawthorns at the start of the season. But this time they subdued the red half of Merseyside with a headed Astle equaliser that took the tie into a third match.

And it was at neutral Manchester City on a Thursday night in mid-April that Albion again displayed their magnificent battling spirit, pinching an early lead through Astle and then withstanding wave after wave of pressure from Bill Shankly's team of warm favourites.

An equaliser inevitably came from Tony Hateley before half-time but Albion, with John Kaye a bloodied hero after a gash to his forehead that required 12 stitches and the wearing of a bandage, went through with Clive Clark's opportunist winner mid-way through the second half.

On to the semi-final at Villa Park against neighbours Birmingham, whom Albion had beaten to win the 1931 Final at Wembley. And this all-West Midlands showdown was marked by a courageous effort from Second Division Blues.

They were probably the better side, certainly in terms of goal attempts, but Albion were starting to believe their name was on the Cup as they went through 2-0 thanks to goals against the run of play by Astle and Tony Brown early in each half.

Everton booked their place at the twin towers too and had done the double over Albion in the League, spectacularly winning 6-2 at The Hawthorns as recently as the March.

But the Throstles, again in their lucky all-white change strip, turned the form-book on its head once more in a final that may not have thrilled the neutral millions, but which will live long in Hawthorns memory.

Chances were few and far between under leaden grey skies in the opening 90 minutes and, as sunshine greeted the start of extra-time, there seemed nothing on when Astle smacked a shot from long range against the body of Everton left-half Colin Harvey at close quarters. But the loose ball fell invitingly on to Astle's left foot and a stunning strike from outside the area whistled into the top far corner with 'keeper Gordon West motionless.

Twenty-seven minutes remained for Albion to hold out after that 93rd minute breakthrough and they did so despite having lost the injured Kaye, the departure of the warhorse striker-turned-defender enabling Dennis Clarke to become the first substitute used in an FA Cup Final.

So it was Albion, led by Williams and inspired by Astle with the proud record of scoring in every round of the competition, who triumphed. They stepped up to receive the famous trophy from Princess Alexandra, who had been jeered by Everton fans during the pre-match formalities because she wore a red outfit matching the colours of arch-rivals Liverpool!

It was Albion's fifth FA Cup Final triumph and was immediately followed by a stormy tour of East Africa – and then by more heroics.

A thrilling Cup defence in 1968-69 was surprisingly ended three minutes from the end of a Hillsborough semi-final by Willenhall-born Allan Clarke. He fired Leicester to a Wembley date (and ultimately defeat) against Manchester City after the smart pre-semi money had been on another Albion v Everton Final.

If Albion, who had included Arsenal (at home) and Chelsea (away) in their list of earlier victims, were a major FA Cup force at the time, though, then they were the dominant club in the League Cup.

In their first year of entering the optional new competition, they lifted the trophy in 1965-66. In their second, they led 2-0 against QPR in the Final at Wembley, only to lose 3-2. In their fifth, they were back at football's mecca, but this time lost to Manchester City.

Goals were certainly the name of their game in those ground-breaking days; three at home to plucky Walsall in round two in 1965-66, four at Leeds in the third round and then six – including an Astle hat-trick – in a fourth-round replay against Coventry. Once Aston Villa had been sent packing 3-1 in the quarter-final, only Peterborough stood between Albion and the Final, and the underdogs kept the first-leg deficit from The Hawthorns to 2-1 before going down 4-2 in the return, with Tony Brown scoring three.

Albion were off to London for the Final, but to Upton Park, not Wembley. The competition had its final two rounds contested over two legs in those days and, after West Ham had inched to a 2-1 half-way lead despite Astle's goal, Jimmy Hagan's side turned on a wonderful attacking exhibition in the return.

They were 4-0 up at the interval through Kaye, Brown, Clark and Williams and, in front of a 32,000 crowd, even a goal by Martin Peters made the aggregate scoreline only 5-3. The club had their first honour for 12 years and had booked their opening excursion into European competition.

The League Cup continued to be both kind and goal-filled. In 1966-67, Villa were humiliated 6-1 at The Hawthorns, Bobby Hope scoring a hat-trick, Manchester City lost 4-2, then lower-division duo Swindon and Northampton were comfortably taken care of on their home grounds.

Who should again stand in Albion's way at the semi-final stage but West Ham! And again the West Bromwich lights proved inspirational as the Hammers were routed 4-0, an Astle hat-trick making the second leg a largely irrelevant 2-2 draw.

With QPR having beaten Birmingham in the other semi-final, Albion were hot favourites – much more so after 'Chippy' Clark had shot them decisively in front at half-time with two goals against his former club. But Albion, by design or accident, eased up and backed off in the second half and were embarrassed as Alec Stock's Third Division side were lifted by Rodney Marsh to a match-winning fightback.

Hagan departed shortly afterwards and was replaced by Alan Ashman. But there was no let-up in the Baggies' cavalier cup exploits. They followed two memorable FA Cup years by rising to the League Cup occasion again in 1969-70, helped on their way by yet another victory over Villa, this time away.

Ipswich and Bradford City were despatched, then Albion got some revenge over their FA Cup conquerors Leicester with a fifth-round replay win. Little Carlisle, the club Ashman had previously managed and was to manage again, were presented as semi-final opponents and were put in their place 4-2 on aggregate despite winning the first leg in Cumbria 1-0.

That success sent Albion off to Wembley to face Manchester City, the two clubs having shared some interesting battles in the previous two or three years. City won the League in 1967-68 despite suffering a double Christmas-time defeat against Albion, who then crashed 6-1 in the Charity Shield at Maine Road at the start of the following season.

A few weeks before Wembley, Albion had won 3-0 in the First Division at home to the team stylishly fashioned by Joe Mercer and Malcolm Allison but that counted for little on Cup Final day despite a headed goal by Astle in the opening minutes. Back came City to level through Mike Doyle and then win it in extra-time through Glyn Pardoe.

That was the end of a great era for Albion. Ashman was sacked while on holiday in the summer of 1971 and the club have not reached a major Final since. Nor have they again played in front of a bigger gate than the one of 97,963 who watched that City clash. With today's smaller stadiums and no standing room, they probably never will.

It looks like a Clive Clark goal but the winger is only following up just in case as Jeff Astle's header goes in for Albion's point-saver at an under-redevelopment Villa Park in October, 1965. The 'building site' is the area now occupied by the Doug Ellis Stand.

Aerial combat. Albion's stand-in 'keeper Rick Sheppard flies off his line to punch clear from Tottenham's Alan Gilzean during the 2-1 defeat at White Hart Lane on October 30, 1965. Also pictured are (from left) John Kaye, Stan Jones, Ray Fairfax and Bobby Hope.

Right-back Bobby Cram waits to pick up the pieces as Albion come under pressure in their 2-2 draw at Anfield on January 15, 1966. Liverpool's No 9 is Ian St John, with the loose ball heading towards Graham Lovett. A fortnight earlier, Albion had launched the New Year with a 5-1 win at Sunderland.

A familiar FA Cup failure. Stan Jones heads away from Welsh international striker Wyn Davies as Albion go out 3-0 in the third round at Second Division Bolton in 1965-66. In five successive seasons starting in 1962-63, they made it no further than round four, then it all came spectacularly right in 1967-68. *Picture by courtesy of the Bolton Evening News.*

Clive Clark nets a typically opportunist equaliser in Albion's 1-1 home draw with Northampton on February 26, 1966. The Cobblers went straight through the divisions to reach the top flight. But their stay was for one year only and they descended almost as quickly.

Celebration time for Albion as they toast the winning of the 1965-66 Football League Cup in the first season they entered it. West Ham were their victims by the emphatic margin of 5-3 over the two legs of the Final, after which the 'party' started. Graham Williams receives the trophy and shows it off to the Hawthorns crowd.

Then the silverware does the rounds in the happy home dressing-room.

Finally, skipper Williams takes the club's prize with him into the bath for safe keeping.

Albion's defence of the League Cup should have been a successful one. They made it to the Final again a year later, this time at Wembley, where they met Third Division QPR. Goals by Clive Clark, seen here beating Rangers 'keeper Peter Springett, gave the favourites a 2-0 interval lead but they collapsed horribly after the break to lose 3-2.

Dogged work from 'keeper John Osborne frustrates Liverpool striker Alf Arrowsmith and sets the agenda for relegation-threatened Albion's shock 1-0 win at Anfield on April 22, 1967. Goalscorer Jeff Astle is in the background, along with Graham Williams, Roger Hunt and Tony Brown.

Another one for the Astle collection. 'King Jeff' swings his left foot and beats Blackpool 'keeper Thomas in Albion's 3-1 win at Bloomfield Road in the club's final First Division away match of 1966-67. Albion had just fired Jimmy Hagan despite their successful battle against relegation and the team were selected by chairman Jim Gaunt and fellow-director Tommy Glidden. Blackpool had long since been condemned to the drop.

Elm Park disease! Reading winger George Harris squeezes in a close-range shot despite the attentions of Eddie Colquhoun, John Osborne, Doug Fraser and last man John Talbut to set Albion on the way to an embarrassing 3-1 League Cup second-round defeat in September, 1967. It was the club's last cup defeat of new manager Alan Ashman's first season. *Picture by courtesy of the Reading Evening Post.*

Eddie Colquhoun, Doug Fraser and John Talbut look on anxiously as Allan Clarke flashes a shot goalwards on Albion's League visit to Fulham on October 7, 1967. Goals by the 'old firm' of Astle and Brown sealed a 2-1 victory – the club's first away success in Division One that season.

The Kop are about to explode in delight as Roger Hunt beats John Osborne to score in Liverpool's 4-1 League victory over Albion in the clubs' first League game of 1968. John Talbut and Graham Williams are also powerless to intervene. Albion had a fine record at Anfield, winning 3-0 there in 1965, 1-0 in 1967 and having three draws during the 1960s as well an epic drawn FA Cup battle.

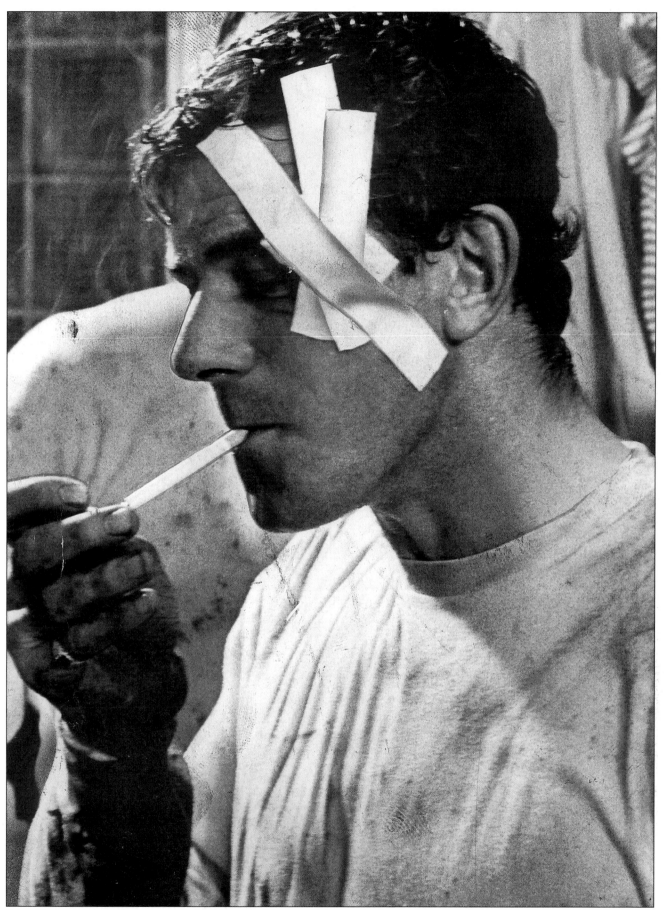

John Kaye, one of Albion's bloodied Maine Road heroes, lights up in the dressing-room after the 2-1 FA Cup sixth-round victory in 1968 over star-studded Liverpool. The game was played at neutral Maine Road after the clubs had drawn 0-0 at The Hawthorns and 1-1 at Anfield. Kaye was successfully converted several months earlier from a striker to a central defender.

Sheffield Wednesday 'keeper Ron Springett leaps to palm the ball to safety away from Jeff Astle, Kenny Stephens and Tony Brown during the 1-1 First Division draw on Easter Saturday, 1968. Holiday time was busier then. Albion had drawn 2-2 at Newcastle the day before.

Birmingham, in particular 'keeper Jim Herriott, are put to the sword as Jeff Astle opens the scoring in the 13th minute of the 1967-68 FA Cup semi-final at Villa Park. Tony Brown drove in the killer second goal after half-time as Albion reached the third of their four major Cup Finals in the space of five and a bit seasons.

John Kaye swings his left boot to spell more problems for Blues' defence but an offside decision came to the rescue of the Second Division battlers on this occasion.

The big day! John Osborne shows a clean pair of hands to deny Everton's Jimmy Husband in the FA Cup Final at Wembley while John Kaye offers support from the rear. *Bottom:* The same duo are safely in position again as John Hurst closes in on goal.

Jeff Astle, a tower of strength for Albion in the air for a decade, threatens the Merseysiders' goal but is beaten from this corner by Brian Labone, with Clive Clark and Tommy Wright in attendance.

In she flies! Everton 'keeper Gordon West is powerless to stop Jeff Astle's 20-yard shot rocketing into the top corner of his net three minutes into extra-time. The goal meant Albion had won the FA Cup for the fifth time and gave Astle the honour of having scored in every round of the competition.

Let the celebrations begin. Astle heads off towards Albion's delirious supporters, eagerly pursued by winger Clive Clark.

Graham Lovett, the baby of the Albion side and brave enough to have resumed his football career after two serious road accidents, aims goalwards again. But Gordon West and England World Cup Final left-back Ray Wilson need not have worried. The whistle had already blown for offside.

Traditional FA Cup winners' pose, 1960s-style. No advertising hoardings or singalongs, just a happy group of players starting to appreciate what they had achieved. Back row (from left): Doug Fraser, Dennis Clarke (the first substitute used in an FA Cup Final), John Osborne, Tony Brown, Graham Lovett, Jeff Astle, John Talbut. Front row: Ian Collard, Graham Williams, Clive Clark, Bobby Hope. Absent from the picture is John Kaye, who had gone off injured before extra-time.

Maine Road misery. Dick Kryzwicki, later to score Albion's goal, gives chase in the 6-1 FA Charity Shield hammering at League champions Manchester City in August, 1968. It was an ill-fated afternoon for Albion, who lost 'keeper John Osborne with a finger injury, Graham Williams taking over in goal. It was the club's fourth Charity Shield appearance. They won 2-0 at Tottenham in 1920, lost 1-0 to Arsenal at Villa Park in 1931 and drew 4-4 with Wolves at Molineux in 1954 thanks to a Ronnie Allen hat-trick.

Welcome home! Skipper Graham Williams shows off the spoils of Albion's success after the squad had returned to West Bromwich just before an end-of-season tour to East Africa.

For a few dizzy months either side of Albion's FA Cup Final triumph, Manchester United were little more than whipping-boys for Alan Ashman's goal-happy team. In April, 1968, shortly before United's European Cup Final triumph, Jeff Astle scored a Hawthorns hat-trick in a remarkable 6-3 home win. In August of the following season, Astle included this header over Alex Stepney in a brace as Albion won 3-1.

European football returned to The Hawthorns in 1968-69, two years after the club's brief assault on the Fairs Cup. This time it was the European Cup-winners' Cup, which threw up a first-round clash with the robust Belgian side, Bruges. Above: Clive Clark is narrowly beaten to the ball by the visiting 'keeper. Below: Jeff Astle suffers the same fate as he takes the aerial route but Albion scored two first-half goals to turn a 3-1 first-leg defeat into overall victory on away goals.

Next stop Rumania. From Bruges, it was on to Bucharest for Albion in the Cup Winners' Cup in November, 1968. Winger Ronnie Rees was sent off in this away leg, where Jeff Astle and John Talbut tested the Dinamo 'keeper in the air. Asa Hartford's goal earned the Baggies a 1-1 draw, which they fully capitalised on by winning 4-0 in the return.

Portman Road pounding. John Kaye's determined challenge fails to stop Colin Viljoen firing home one of the Ipswich goals in their 4-1 win over Albion on December 7, 1968. *Picture by courtesy of the Norwich Evening News.*

The start of a strong defence of the FA Cup. Jeff Astle, later to convert his only Albion penalty, floats a header just over the bar in January, 1969, as the holders beat Norwich 3-0 in the third round of the competition they had won eight months earlier.

Fulham and England star Johnny Haynes is denied from point-blank range by John Osborne in Albion's 2-1 FA Cup fourth-round win at Craven Cottage in January, 1969. The Cottagers had Albion under fierce pressure in the second half but were sunk by goals from Asa Hartford and Ronnie Rees. *Picture courtesy of Ken Coton.*

Cup-tie tension as Albion players John Kaye (No 6) and goalscorer Jeff Astle converge on Peter Osgood following a challenge on 'keeper John Osborne in the dying minutes of the quarter-final 2-1 win at Chelsea in March, 1969. John Talbut is the player going to Osborne's assistance.

No prizes for guessing who won and who lost. Albion's 'lucky' all-white change strip let them down on this occasion – the FA Cup semi-final against Leicester at Hillsborough in the spring of 1969. The only goal of the game came three minutes from time from the foot of Willenhall-born Allan Clarke after Albion had beaten Arenal in round five and Chelsea away in the quarter-final.

One of cup football's more spectacular collapses. Albion players are consoled by trainer Jimmy Dunn after seeing a 3-0 first-leg victory turned into a 6-3 aggregate defeat against Sunderland in the Final of the 1968-69 FA Youth Cup. Albion had Asa Hartford and the late Jim Holton sent off in a thoroughly miserable return at Roker Park, where Lyndon Hughes (crouching), Dave Butler, No 9 Keith Morton, 'keeper Gordon Nisbet and No 11 Hugh MacLean display their dejection while the Wearsiders parade the silverware.

A unique occasion; Coventry 3 Albion 1 at Highfield Road in August, 1969. The game was Gordon Nisbet's only first-team match in the goalkeeper role in which he launched his career. He later went on to make many hundred appearances for his various clubs as a right-back. *Above:* Nisbet is on his knees and Graham Williams is on the line, neither of them able to keep out a Willie Carr goal which helped give the Sky Blues maximum points in this first midweek of the season. *Below:* Better luck for the debutant 'keeper as he punches clear watched by team-mates Williams, John Kaye and Jeff Astle. *Pictures courtesy of the Coventry Evening Telegraph.*

No way through. Dick Kryzwicki runs out of space as he tries to sidestep John Robson and Dave Mackay in Albion's 2-0 First Division home defeat against Derby in August, 1969.

Doug Fraser is the meat in the Roker Park sandwich as 'keeper Jim Cumbes leaves his line to try to punch clear in Albion's 2-2 draw against Sunderland on September 6, 1969.

All-out effort from John Kaye as he challenges substitute John Boyle in the League game at Chelsea in October, 1969. Seven months earlier, Albion had won at Stamford Bridge in the FA Cup quarter-final but they lost 2-0 on this occasion.

More London blues for Albion, this time a fortnight later at Tottenham, where they were beaten 2-0 despite this penalty escape following a joint challenge by Graham Williams and John Talbut.

The Cumbrian Wall. John Talbut, scorer of only one Albion goal in 193 senior appearances, tries his luck in the League Cup semi-final first leg against Carlisle at Brunton Park in November, 1970. Albion lost 1-0 but stormed through by winning the return 4-1.

One happy Hawthorns dressing-room. Ray Wilson (left) and skipper Doug Fraser bask in the glory of a job well done after Albion had overcome manager Alan Ashman's former club Carlisle to book their return to Wembley.

May the best team win. Doug Fraser and his Manchester City counterpart Tony Book exchange pleasantries before the Final on March 7, 1970. As well as Carlisle, Albion had beaten Villa (away), Ipswich (in a home replay), Bradford City (home) and Leicester (in a home replay) on their League Cup journey.

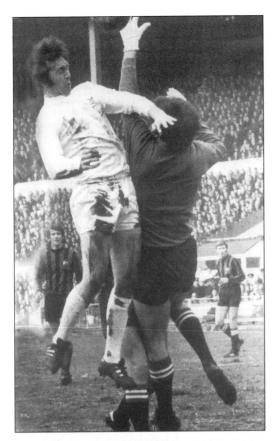

The perfect start. Jeff Astle beats Joe Corrigan in the air to nod Albion in front after only seven minutes and become the first man to score in Wembley finals of both the FA Cup and League Cup.

John Osborne goes down to hold a low cross under pressure from City winger Mike Summerbee as Ray Wilson keeps watch.

Francis Lee on the rampage. *Above*, he and No 11 Glyn Pardoe require the attention of Len Cantello, Ray Wilson, a grounded John Talbut and John Kaye. *Picture by courtesy of the Manchester Evening News. Below*: The England forward powers in a header.

On a pitch badly churned up following midweek snow and the staging of the Horse of the Year show, Albion's resistance finally ended with a Mike Doyle equaliser in the second half. Keeper Osborne cuts an understandably dejected figure as his team-mates prepare for the restart. *Picture by courtesy of the Manchester Evening News.*

A great chance goes begging. Colin Suggett, Albion's record signing when bought from Sunderland for £100,000 the previous summer, slices wide when faced with only Corrigan to beat. *Picture by courtesy of the Manchester Evening News.*

The decider. Glyn Pardoe lunges in slightly ahead of Fraser and Osborne to touch in City's extra-time winner. The side moulded by Joe Mercer and Malcolm Allison had won the League, the FA Cup and the Charity Shield in the previous two years and went on to win the European Cup-winners' Cup a few weeks later.

End of an era. Albion's players troop along the Royal Box with only hard-luck stories to console them after their 2-1 defeat. Little would supporters who had enjoyed three visits to the twin towers in three and a bit years have believed that it would be well over two decades before the club returned to the national stadium.

A case of nearly but not quite following Albion's return to First Division action. Burnley 'keeper Peter Mellor keeps his goal intact despite Colin Suggett's presence in the opening minutes of a 1-1 draw in a Turf Moor mudbath on March 21, 1970.

John Osborne deals with this Everton attack but the blue tide was remorseless at Goodison Park in front of a near-60,000 crowd on the night of April 2, 1970. Harry Catterick's side, including Howard Kendall (right), won 2-0 and so clinched the First Division championship. Albion players pictured are (from left) a young Alistair Robertson, Doug Fraser, Lyndon Hughes and Alan Merrick.

Revenge in the making. Nobby Stiles closes in on John Osborne's goal, watched by Ray Wilson, Alistair Robertson, Bobby Hope, Alan Merrick and Lyndon Hughes, during Albion's nightmare 7-0 crash at Old Trafford in April, 1970. Manchester United's crushing victory avenged the defeats they had suffered by 6-3, 3-1 and 2-1 at The Hawthorns in three trips from April, 1968.

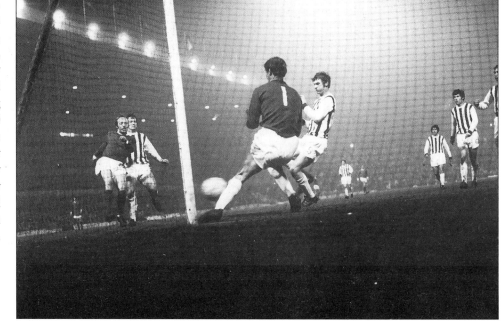

Ups and Downs

The chase is on. Bobby Hope pursues the in-possession Peter Cormack during the 3-3 draw at Nottingham Forest in Albion's first away game of 1970-71.

Jim Cumbes, watched by John Kaye and No 6 Alan Merrick, clutches a low shot in Albion's Texaco Cup clash at Morton in September, 1970. The Scots won 2-1 north of the border and 1-0 in the second leg.

A goal-den moment for Colin Suggett as he heads past Peter Grotier, in front of a watching Bobby Moore, for a late winner against West Ham in September, 1970. It was the second goal of the game for the striker.

Nearly another Suggett goal but he is foiled by a flying save from Derby 'keeper Les Green. Albion nevertheless emerged triumphant 2-1 from this early-season First Division clash at The Hawthorns.

Winger George McVitie turns the ball past Gary Sprake from close range in Albion's 2-2 draw with Leeds on October 10, 1970. Later that season, Leeds were to find Albion a surprise barrier to their hopes of lifting the League title.

Jim Cumbes to the rescue. But the 'keeper's save from Bobby Tambling on this occasion, witnessed by a backpedalling John Kaye and Alan Merrick, failed to save Albion from a 3-0 beating at Crystal Palace.

By the time Albion suffered this 2-1 November defeat against newly-promoted Huddersfield at Leeds Road, they had become poor travellers, going nearly a year without an away League win. Here, Alan Merrick clears from Brian Greenhalgh, with Tony Brown keeping an eye on proceedings. *Picture by courtesy of the Huddersfield Examiner.*

No way past Great Gordon. Colin Suggett beats Stoke right-back John Marsh with an overhead kick but Albion still drew a blank against England 'keeper Gordon Banks in this 2-0 defeat at the Victoria Ground in January, 1971.

Stormy scenes at Elland Road after the infamous Jeff Astle goal which Leeds blamed for losing the 1970-71 championship to Arsenal. The controversy, accompanied by crowd trouble and some strong words here involving referee Ray Tinkler, Billy Bremner, John Wile and Mick Jones, overshadowed a brilliant Albion performance. The 2-1 mid-April win was their first away in the First Division in 28 trips going back a year and four months.

And then Albion dealt a setback for Leeds' title rivals Arsenal! A week after their Elland Road heroics, Albion held the Gunners 2-2 at The Hawthorns thanks to this clinical Asa Hartford finish between Frank McLintock and Bob Wilson. But Arsenal recovered to win the League and FA Cup double.

Crossing the international borders. John Kaye greets Inter Milan skipper Mazzolla before the Anglo Italian Cup clash at The Hawthorns in the summer of 1971. Albion, having competed with reaasonable success against Roma and Lanerossi Vicenza the previous year, drew 1-1 with Inter and lost the return 1-0. They also lost by the odd goal home and away against Cagliari.

New season, new manager. Alan Ashman was sacked in the summer of 1971 and his successor Don Howe, the former Albion full-back, was quick to preach his message. No 11 Asa Hartford is on the receiving end here, with Jeff Astle gaining an 'overview.'

Wrexham was Albion's first destination during their excursion into the Watney Cup in the warm-up to 1971-72. Jeff Astle and Tony Brown lead this assault on the Welshmen's goal, Brown scoring twice for a side who then beat Halifax away before losing on penalties in the Final at home to Colchester.

There was a marked emphasis on defence during the Howe reign and Jeff Astle found himself a bystander in this training-ground routine as John Kaye and Lyndon Hughes come face-to-face.

Misery against Manchester United – in the Potteries. Ray Wilson, John Kaye, Len Cantello, Tony Brown, Jeff Astle and grounded 'keeper Jim Cumbes share the same despondent look as United celebrate a goal by Alan Gowling in August, 1971. The Monday night game, which featured a brilliant two-goal performance by George Best and brought Albion their first defeat under their new boss, was played at Stoke as a punishment for United, following crowd trouble at their earlier games.

Another away defeat, this time at Chelsea on September 1, 1971. A new Brazilian-style change strip coincided with some highly indifferent performances, although John Wile's presence in this attack at Stamford Bridge worried John Dempsey, Peter Osgood and 'keeper John Phillips.

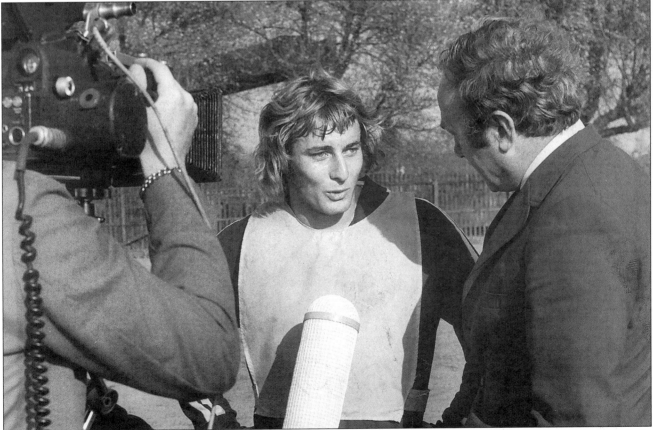

In the spotlight. Asa Hartford is interviewed by ATV Sport's Billy Wright after agreeing a £170,000 move to Leeds in November, 1971. But the Scot's world fell in hours later when his transfer was scuppered by the revelation that he had a hole in the heart.

Instead of going into action for a Don Revie team chasing the double, Hartford was sent back to The Hawthorns and returned to Albion's line-up just over a week later – for this 4-1 defeat at Nottingham Forest.

Albion went into the New Year facing an uphill battle against relegation – a fight that became even tougher when, despite this effort from Bobby Gould, they lost 2-1 at Everton on January 22, 1972.

A Hawthorns pea-souper! Heavy snow and thick mud marked Albion's home clash with Nottingham Forest on March 4. But there were no complaints as they ground out a crucial 1-0 win. Albion stayed up and Forest, who had Doug Fraser in their line-up, didn't.

All packed up and ready to go. Albion's players wait to board the coach taking them to the airport for their pre-season tour of Holland in July, 1972. Left to right are Lyndon Hughes, Tony Brown, Asa Hartford, George McVitie, on-loan 'keeper John Farmer, Ray Wilson, John Wile and Bobby Gould.

Picture with a difference. Asa Hartford, who had almost joined Leeds the previous season, chases Billy Bremner in Albion's 2-0 defeat at Elland Road early in their 1972-73 relegation year. John Wile and Alistair Robertson, who amassed nearly 1,250 appearances for the club between them, are powerless to intervene. And the difference? Albion are wearing a borrowed change strip from their opponents.

End of a grim run. This Tony Brown effort was disallowed in the First Division draw at Newcastle on August 23, 1972. But Alistair Brown used the same game to score the first goal of Albion's season – in their fourth match.

A Latchford family gathering. Albion 'keeper Peter hangs on as Birmingham striker Bob towers over him in the 2-2 Hawthorns draw on August 30, 1972. A third brother, Dave, was in goal for newly-promoted Blues.

Lean times looming. Alistair Brown is denied by a clearance from Henry Newton in Albion's 1-0 September defeat at Everton – a game that confirmed they were in for a season of First Division struggle.

An off-duty Peter Latchford, hanging around at Dudley Zoo with a monkey hanging around him. The former schoolboy basketball international played under-21 football for England as well and, after making 104 senior appearances for Albion, included a 'Player of the Year' award in his long service to Celtic.

Proud moment for Asa Hartford as he receives his Scottish cap from Albion chairman Jim Gaunt, watched by his team-mates and manager Don Howe. The midfielder who had failed a Leeds medical went on to play 50 full internationals for his country and feature in some 900 matches for his various clubs!

Kings at the Palace. Alistair Brown and John Wile lead this attack on the Crystal Palace goal during Albion's 2-0 victory at Selhurst Park on September 16, 1972.

Unusual Stamford Bridge backcloth for Albion's 3-1 defeat against Chelsea on October 14, 1972 – a time when the London club were rebuilding their main stand. Here, Colin Suggett (left) and Bobby Gould are allowed a free joint header by Ron Harris.

John Wile heads away from Brian O'Neill but almost into the path of No 8 Mike Channon as Albion's battle to beat the drop suffers this 2-1 autumn-time defeat against Southampton at The Dell. Alistair Robertson, Asa Hartford and Roger Minton are the other yellow-shirted players in view.

End to the marathon. Colin Suggett and John Wile both seem to have made contact but Suggett was credited with this FA Cup goal against Nottingham Forest at neutral Leicester. The third-round tie went to Filbert Street at the fourth time of asking after the sides had drawn at The Hawthorns and the City Ground and had the original replay curtailed by fog. Albion eventually won 3-1 but went out at Leeds in round five. On the left is Martin O'Neill, later to manage Leicester.

Sliding fast. Two more points go begging as Albion are beaten 2-0 at Ipswich on March 17, 1973. Here, Ray Wilson leaves the coast clear for John Osborne to take the ball off the head of Ipswich's David Johnson.

A ray of hope. Victory at home to Leicester at the start of April, despite a rare penalty miss by Tony Brown, kept Albion in the survival hunt, although Jeff Astle (right) and Don Howe's signings David Shaw (left) and Willie Johnston couldn't find a way through here.

The end is nigh. David Shaw flashes a left-wing centre across Tommy Smith but Albion's safety-first performance at Anfield was punished by a 1-0 April 14 defeat, sealed by an early Kevin Keegan penalty.

The defeat that effectively spelled relegation. Albion 0 Norwich 1 on April 21. John Osborne pushes over with Canaries sub Paul Cheesley in attendance but the game was a massive one in the struggle to stay up. Norwich did and Albion didn't, the Baggies' demise ending their proud 24-year unbroken run as a First Division club. *Picture by courtesy of the Norwich Evening News.*

A star groundsman. Jeff Astle takes time out to help unroll the new turf that Albion laid in the summer of 1973 as they prepared for Second Division football. It was to be Astle's tenth and last season at The Hawthorns.

Counting the cost of the drop. Tony Brown's free-kick flashes through the Carlisle wall for Albion's equaliser in a 1-1 draw on October 13, 1973. But only 12,556 were present – and things were to get worse. On the far right is former Albion winger Dennis Martin.

Shades of 1968. Six seasons on, Everton and Albion were back in FA Cup combat, drawing 0-0 in a fourth-round tie at Goodison Park, although Asa Hartford flashed this shot past Micky Bernard and just off target. It was Albion's first-ever Sunday game and the first time any English match staged on that day of the week had attracted a 50,000 gate. Albion's first League fixture on a Sunday came a week later at Portsmouth and was also drawn. Second Division Albion won the fourth-round replay against Everton 1-0.

Happy day in an unhappy season. John Wile turns away after opening the scoring in the 3-1 League victory at Villa on March 2, 1974. Jeff Astle (left), starting an Albion game for the last-but-one time, sets off in pursuit of the marksman while Tony Brown joins in the celebrations in a match in which he later scored twice. Don Howe's side faded badly to finish eighth.

Astle's very last competitive game for Albion – and only as a substitute. Peter Latchford's 86th minute penalty save from Gil Reece was a temporary highlight in this 2-2 home draw with Cardiff on March 30, 1974. The kick was ordered to be retaken and this time ex-Birmingham man John Vincent scored.

Defender-turned-midfielder Alan Merrick enjoyed a flurry of goals early in 1974-75 and sealed a 2-0 Hawthorns triumph over York with this strike at the start of October.

Time for a handover. Against the backcloth of Albion's 1968 FA Cup Final winning goal, retiring chairman Jim Gaunt (left) passes on his best wishes to his successor, Bert Millichip, who was to loyally serve both the club and his country in office.

Albion made two losing visits to Norwich in their second season in Division Two, Peter Latchford and Alistair Robertson struggling to contain Ted MacDougall in this 2-0 extra-time defeat in the League Cup in mid-October.

A popular reunion. The Class of '68 were back together on October 30, 1974, when Albion's FA Cup winners were joined by George Best for Jeff Astle's testimonial game. Also pictured are (from left) George McVitie, Ken Foggo, Bobby Hope, Ian Collard, Ray Fairfax, Graham Lovett, Dennis Clarke, John Kaye, John Osborne, Tony Brown, Doug Fraser, Graham Williams.

Six Albion players – Ray Wilson, John Wile, Len Cantello, match-winner Joe Mayo, Alan Glover and Gordon Nisbet – look on as the safe hands of 'keeper John Osborne put an end to a Bolton attack in the 1-0 Second Division victory at Burnden Park in December, 1974. *Picture by courtesy of the Bolton Evening News.*

Riding High

Don Howe was sacked towards the end of a second unappetising Division Two season and replaced several weeks later by Johnny Giles. The club's first player-manager discusses tactics here with (from left) John Trewick, Gordon Nisbet, Bryan Robson and John Wile. Robson made his debut at York several days after Howe's departure and scored in his other two outings before the end of the campaign.

World Cup Final hero Geoff Hurst was one of Albion's surprise signings for 1975-76 and found the target in this early-season 2-2 draw at home to York.

Ron Harris a hard-man? 'Chopper' dons his gloves for Chelsea's Second Division clash with Albion on January 31, 1976! Albion, inspired here by Mick Martin, underlined their promotion challenge with a 2-1 win at Stamford Bridge.

Wise-cracking Willie Johnston seems to be asking for liquid refreshment as team-mate Joe Mayo, watched over by No 3 Bryan Robson, receives treatment during Albion's vital 2-0 victory over promotion rivals Bolton on March 20. In the middle of the Bolton trio is Peter Reid.

Jeff Astle struck with his left foot at Wembley in 1968 and Tony Brown followed suit on this high-pressure occasion at Oldham on April 24, 1976. Brown's venomous volley just before the hour, after Ally Brown had helped back a right-wing cross by Paddy Mulligan, broke a tense deadlock and gave Albion the win they needed to end three years of exile in the Second Division.

Tony Brown, born a few hundred yards from Oldham's Boundary Park ground, is converged on by Paddy Mulligan, Willie Johnston, Alistair Robertson and Len Cantello after the most important goal of the 279 he managed in his Albion career.

They're up! Cantello, Mulligan, Ally Brown, John Wile and, in the distance, 'keeper John Osborne, who was an ever-present in 1975-76, start the sprint for the dressing-room in a bid to beat the invasion of the pitch by sections of Albion's massive 15,000 following.

Let the celebrations begin! Out comes the bubbly, poured by chairman Bert Millichip and enjoyed by player-manager Johnny Giles, Alistair Robertson, John Wile and Willie Johnston. A few weeks later, Giles resigned, claiming dissatisfaction at the lot of the manager. But he was persuaded to stay on for another season.

While the first team were soaring, the club's youngsters were on their way to lifting the FA Youth Cup for the first time. In the Final, they beat Wolves 2-0 away and 3-0 at home.

Champagne time in the bath for Albion youth skipper Wayne Hughes as he savours success at a stage of the competition that Albion had twice failed at – in 1955 against Manchester United and in 1969 against Sunderland.

Warming up for the top flight. Willie Johnston is on the ball in training in the summer of 1976, surrounded by Joe Mayo, Paddy Mulligan, Alistair Robertson and John Trewick.

Traditional symbol of The Hawthorns. The famous throstle was 'perched' for many years on top of the old scoreboard in the Woodman Corner of the ground. It is seen here getting a touch-up from West Bromwich signwriter John Imm but disappeared from public view with the ground redevelopment of the 1990s. It then 'came to rest' in the opposite corner of the stadium.

The final countdown …Albion's pre-season programme took them into a warm-up game at Nottingham Forest in the Midland group of the Anglo Scottish Cup. Joe Mayo is closely watched here by Frank Clark – later to become Forest's boss – in Albion's 3-2 defeat.

Back in the big time. Albion's brilliant Scottish international winger Willie Johnston wriggles past Leeds' Trevor Cherry in the 2-2 draw at Elland Road that launched the club's impressive return to Division One.

The strange story of Ray Treacy. The Republic of Ireland forward scored on his debut for the club at Sunderland in 1966. When Johnny Giles took him back to The Hawthorns ten years later, Treacy obliged with this goal and another on his second 'debut' in a draw at Derby.

'Bomber' alert! Tony Brown, who turned down an apprenticeship at Old Trafford because he thought he would be given a better chance at Albion, rubs shoulders with Brian Greenhoff in his side's 4-0 trouncing of Manchester United on October 16, 1976. A year later, they again beat them 4-0.

More shades of Manchester United, this time provided by a George Best goal for Wolves at Molineux in Mike Bailey's testimonial in the autumn of 1976.

White hell for Albion as Mick Martin misses one of their chances in a 1-0 FA Cup third-round exit at home to Manchester City in January, 1977. Willie Johnston had scored in the drawn first clash at Maine Road.

What a start! Laurie Cunningham, signed from Orient shortly before, fires home Albion's first goal in their 2-1 First Division victory against Middlesbrough on April 2, 1977.

A five-star show! Mick Martin beats Leicester 'keeper Mark Wallington as Albion run riot to the tune of a 5-0 romp on their visit to Filbert Street in May, 1977. The club just missed a UEFA Cup spot in their first season back up but the idolised Johnny Giles duly quit in the summer.

Albion 2 Rangers 0 at Ibrox Park. That was the result when the side by now managed by Ronnie Allen went north of the border in the summer of 1977 to compete in the Tennent-Caledonian Cup. Mick Martin missed the 4-3 semi-final win over St Mirren but is pictured here in possession in the Final.

It's ours. Albion players, led by skipper John Wile, are quietly contented rather than outwardly jubilant at having defeated the Scottish giants in their own backyard.

Away to a flier. David Cross, who had two spells at The Hawthorns, lashes home to round off the scoring in the 3-0 win over Chelsea on the first day of the 1977-78 campaign.

Wing wizardry from Willie Johnston as he torments Malcolm Page and Gary Emmanuel in Albion's 3-1 win at home to Birmingham on September 24, 1977.

Wolves were also at The Hawthorns in September and, after this David Cross goal, were thankful to escape with a 2-2 draw at a time when Albion were inspired by a new boy called Cyrille Regis.

Ayresome Park, so often a graveyard for Albion hopes, proved unlucky again on January 21, 1978, in the early days of Ron Atkinson's first reign as Hawthorns boss. Boro won 1-0 despite this aerial assault by John Wile and Cyrille Regis against Stuart Boam and Alan Ramage. *Picture by courtesy of the North-East Evening Gazette, Middlesbrough.*

Now, how did the others get on in the League? Alistair Robertson displays a look of rugged satisfaction as he checks on First Division results following the victory that put Albion in yet another FA Cup semi-final. With him is Mick Martin.

One of the many famous Cyrille Regis goals. This right-foot fizzer flashed past Peter Shilton to give Albion a 2-0 Hawthorns triumph over Brian Clough's title-bound Nottingham Forest in the quarter-final of the 1977-78 FA Cup.

Off to Highbury! More than 20,000 Albion fans set off down the M1 on April 8, 1978, confident of victory over Ipswich and therefore another trip to London a few weeks later. But the day didn't go according to plan …

The bloodied hero. John Wile suffered a serious gashed forehead in trying to prevent Brian Talbot's early goal for Bobby Robson's underdogs. The skipper and centre-half continued with headband, gave his lot, but finally had to admit defeat as he went off in the second half of Ipswich's 3-1 success.

The dream is over. Tony Brown, who had briefly revived Albion's hopes by converting a penalty in front of the club's supporters packed in Highbury's North Bank, trudges off, followed by Wile. To complete a black day, Albion had Mick Martin sent off.

Despite Cup elimination, Albion still made it into Europe, helped by this 3-1 victory at Manchester City a week later. Laurie Cunningham is about to pounce following a half-save from Joe Corrigan.

Not what it seems. Tony Brown, who scored more than 50 penalties for Albion, actually missed this one against Everton's George Wood in the club's penultimate home match of the season. But the Merseysiders were beaten 3-1 anyway, with Cyrille Regis scoring twice.

Albion were never short of invites to travel abroad in Ron Atkinson's time. In 1978, they became the first English professional club to tour China, where secretary Alan Everiss (right) and director Brian Boundy were keen to see the Great Wall.

Tom Silk (left) and Bert Millichip (second left) are full of Oriental curiosity as they prepare to take their seats on match-day. Albion played in front of crowds of 80,000, 89,400, 40,000, 30,500 and 18,000 as they won five matches out of five, the last of them in Hong Kong.

Three familiar Hawthorns faces of the late 1970s – and one surprise figure – seen here during pre-season training in July 1978. From left to right are Laurie Cunningham, Cyrille Regis, Brendon Batson and Bruce Grobbelaar, the latter then a 20-year-old triallist about to find his way in the English game with Crewe and, of course, Liverpool.

Home in shame. Willie Johnston is met by manager Ron Atkinson and ushered through Heathrow's customs by police after being banished in disgrace from the 1978 World Cup Finals in Argentina. Johnston, then 31, admitted illegally taking two pep-pills and was banned for life from playing for Scotland, for whom he had won 22 full caps.

Len Cantello and a falling Ally Brown do battle with England midfielder Ray Kennedy during Albion's 1-1 draw with Liverpool on September 23, 1978. The two clubs, deadlocked at The Hawthorns after Kenny Dalglish had embarrassed Tony Godden with an extraordinary equaliser, were to become title rivals in the New Year.

The first of a magnificent seven. Len Cantello flashes a shot past Coventry defender Bobby McDonald to set Albion on the way to a stunning 7-1 home win on October 21, 1978.

A week later, on 28 October 1978, Cyrille Regis beats Manchester City goalkeeper Joe Corrigan to score Albion's first goal in the 2-2 draw at Maine Road.

'Bomber Brown' — Record Breaker

TONY Brown's place in Hawthorns folklore is secure for all time – and his records will probably never be broken.

In these club-hopping days, his statistics sound quite extraordinary – 279 League and Cup goals in 720 competitive first-team appearances.

Apart from W. G. Richardson, whose club record tally of 328 included 100 in wartime football, no other Albion player has scored anything like as many goals, nor played anything like as many matches as he did in just over 20 glorious years at the club.

With friendlies, his appearance tally soared to 818 and his goals total to 312 – not bad for a player who feared as a child that asthma might deny him a professional career!

'Bomber' was born in Oldham in 1945 and joined Albion in 1961 after serving Manchester Schools. His debut came at Ipswich in September, 1963, and typically, he marked the occasion with a goal in a 2-1 win.

September 28, 1963; debut-day for Tony Brown. The 17-year-old Mancunian figured in a small Albion forward line of (left to right) Ken Foggo, Brown, Ronnie Fenton, Alec Jackson and Clive Clark. But 'Bomber' started as he meant to go on, scoring in a 2-1 First Division victory at Ipswich.

Twelve more League appearances and five more First Division goals followed for him in that campaign, including a particularly popular one in a 4-3 home win over Aston Villa.

Goalscorer turns goalkeeper. It's on with the green jersey and time to display a clean pair of hands as he takes over from the injured John Osborne in a First Division defeat at Blackpool in August, 1970.

Sometimes a right-winger, often an inside-right, occasionally a striker but usually an attacking right-half – another reason why his goal tally was so extraordinary – Brown was to give 17 loyal seasons to Albion's first team.

He opened the 1964-65 programme with a goal away to his boyhood Manchester United favourites and followed up with his first Albion hat-trick – in a 4-1 home victory against Sunderland.

He was an established first-teamer by the time Albion

Hat-trick time against Manchester United – the club he could have joined straight from school. These three goals came in a 4-3 League victory on March 6, 1971. First, a characteristic power-drive through a crowd of players including Bobby Charlton, then a steered left-footer from close range that beat Alex Stepney and finally a right-foot shot over the 'keeper despite Tony Dunne's sliding challenge.

won the League Cup in 1965-66, scoring 17 goals in 35 First Division appearances and ten in the thrilling cup run. His contribution to that journey included a semi-final hat-trick at Peterborough, which set the Baggies up for a showdown with West Ham – a clash that ended with a scintillating 4-1 home win and an aggregate 5-3 triumph.

Brown figured in Albion's low-key first-ever excursion into European football in 1966-67, scoring a Hawthorns

Fairs Cup hat-trick against the Dutchmen of DOS Utrecht in the process, and in the same year went with them to Wembley in a second successive League Cup final.

In that campaign, he scored 14 League goals, including hat-tricks at home to Tottenham and Newcastle, and was on target at Northampton in both the League Cup and FA Cup. Alas there was no happy ending beneath the twin towers as Third Division QPR pulled off a shock victory.

Brown, by now confirmed as the club's penalty

A good career move? 'Bomber' beats boss Johnny Giles in training in December, 1976.

specialist – his highly profitable style was based on power rather than placement – was part of successful Albion sides in the FA Cup in 1967-68 and 1968-69, scoring four times in the triumphant Cup campaign that ended gloriously against Everton at Wembley in the former season and getting on the scoresheet another twice before a fine Cup defence ended in semi-final heartbreak against Leicester the following spring.

Brown was voted Midlands Footballer of the Year in 1969 – a feat he repeated in 1971 and 1979 – and, having represented England at youth level (he also played for the Football League side), he picked up his solitary senior cap at home to Wales in 1971.

The goals continued to fly in for

Penalties were commonplace among the goal haul. Hard and true was the philosophy – as with this effort against Chelsea on the opening day of 1977-78.

The protruding tongue was almost an 'ever-present', too! Leicester's David Webb fails to cut out a shot in a 2-0 home win on Bonfire Night afternoon, 1977.

Another penalty, another goal. David Harvey is beaten, so are Leeds, by the only goal of the game on the last day of 1977.

With this effort in a 3-1 win at Chelsea in September, 1978, Tony Brown equalled the record of the man who previously held the record as the club's highest scorer in League matches, Ronnie Allen (208).

him, one in the FA Cup third round at Sheffield Wednesday in January, 1970, still being talked of today – a rasping half-volley from well outside the area after the ball had dropped over his shoulder following a colleague's midfield challenge.

Brown, who had scored against Belgian and Rumanian opposition in the club's journey to the last eight of the 1968-69 European Cup-winners' Cup, also struck twice in the League Cup the following year before Albion lost another final – this time to Manchester City.

Twenty-eight goals in 42 League matches made 1970-71 memorable for him – he was the First Division's leading marksman – then came 17 in 40 the following campaign before he lost his way under the more defensively-minded Don Howe. He even became unsettled at one point.

Albion suffered the misery of relegation in 1973 but Brown – now a first-teamer for ten years – still provided some great memories, notably when he unleashed an FA Cup hat-trick at home to Notts County and a week later

scored all four goals in a League win at Nottingham Forest.

Inevitably, it was his goal on April 24, 1976, that memorably ended the club's three-year stay in the Second Division. The fact the brilliant promotion-clincher was scored at Oldham was even more fitting. He was born just down the road from Boundary Park!

After a couple of quiet seasons goal-wise, Brown was back with a bang in 1977-78 as he rattled in 25 goals, followed by 14 in 1978-79, including both on Albion's finest European occasion – the December night on which they saw off Valencia 2-0 at The Hawthorns to reach the quarter-final of the UEFA Cup. He also scored two of the five with which inspired Albion destroyed Manchester United 5-3 at Old Trafford that Christmas.

It was at Chelsea in the autumn of the same season that Brown had equalled Ronnie Allen's all-time club record of 208 League goals – a mark he moved ahead of with another venomous strike at Leeds a fortnight later.

Sadly, time was catching up with him and the two goals he scored against visiting Coventry in October, 1979, were to be his last in the League for the club. Early in the New Year, he appeared on Albion's score-sheet for the final time in a 2-1 FA Cup replay defeat at West Ham.

Coincidentally, his 561st and last League start for the club was at Ipswich, where he had also made his first more than a decade and a half earlier.

Tony Brown was always an utterly dedicated, wholehearted performer who remained hugely popular with supporters and team-mates – a point underlined when a crowd of around 600 turned up at a testimonial dinner for him as recently as May, 1998. Experienced fans are still dismayed he won only one England cap – against Wales in 1970-71.

In the mid-1980s, he served the club as a coach and now, despite two hip replacements, he remains a home-and-away fan, longing for the day Albion return to the top flight – the place that was lit up by his goals and endeavours for many exciting years.

And, in a 3-1 victory at Leeds a fortnight later, 'Bomber' broke Allen's League record. He went on to finish with 218 League goals in his total League and Cup haul for the club of 279. Only W. G. Richardson had a higher total, his 328 including 100 in wartime.

The European Experience

'PLAY away first' is one of the oft-repeated recipes for European progress. And, in that respect, Albion have been fortunate when crossing paths with their counterparts on the Continent. In all 11 of their ties in recognised international competition, they have travelled first and staged the Hawthorns leg second. What's more, they have not visited the same country twice for ties, be it in the Fairs Cup, the European Cup-winners' Cup or the UEFA Cup.

Five times, the club have qualified for Europe and, in all but the last two of those campaigns, they have made some progress. Indeed, Albion have twice appeared on the brink of a place in the last four. Alas, twice they have then slipped up after drawing the away legs of quarter-finals.

In the 1968-69 European Cup-winners' Cup, they held Dunfermline to a 0-0 draw at East End Park but, on an icy Hawthorns night on which 21 of the 22 players wore gloves, the determined Scots pinched an early goal and then clung to it resolutely.

It was a depressing end to an incident-packed Albion adventure which had started in bizarre style against Bruges of Belgium.

To say Alan Ashman's team of FA Cup winners were roughed up would be putting it mildly. In the away first leg, Jeff Astle was carried off after a blow to the head during a melee that turned into a near-riot featuring baton-wielding police.

The Belgians won 3-1 and immediately made their intentions clear in the return leg as their central defenders meted out some strong-arm stuff to Astle in particular. But Albion kept their cool to win 2-0 thanks to goals by teenager Asa Hartford, who had also scored in Bruges, and Tony Brown to go through on the away goals rule.

On their next trip overseas, Albion had Ronnie Rees given his marching orders. The winger could have few complaints over his dismissal against Dinamo Bucharest in Rumania but the fact the English club remained calm to draw 1-1 thanks to Hartford's third goal in three Euro games was reflected at the final whistle. Stormy crowd scenes around the tunnel prompted the need for a heavy police presence and Albion's players were grateful for their hosts' sporting behaviour in helping usher them off the pitch and to the safety of the dressing-room.

The second leg was a much more straightforward affair.

Four goals, two of them from Tony Brown, and none in reply, sent Albion through to the Anglo Scottish assignment that was to end in disappointment in the New Year.

The supporters had taken to the Cup-winners' Cup in a big way. More than 33,000 watched the home legs of the ties against Bruges and Bucharest and the Dunfermline return was witnessed by only several hundred fewer. It had been a satisfactory journey and a one-round improvement on the club's only previous taste of European competition.

That had come in the 1966-67 Fairs Cup as a reward for Albion's winning of the League Cup. There was more than a little winter chill in the air when the first whistle blew on the opening leg of the second-round clash with DOS Utrecht in Holland – a match from which Jimmy Hagan's men emerged with an untidy 1-1 draw courtesy of Bobby Hope's goal.

Only 5,500 watched the first match but over 19,000 were present to see Brown's hat-trick set up a 5-2 win in the return and a 6-3 aggregate victory.

A three-month wait followed before Albion flew out to Italy to take on talented Bologna, who boasted inside-forward Helmut Haller, West Germany's World Cup Final star, in their ranks. And the class gap was all too obvious in each game as a 3-0 home win was followed by a 3-1 Hawthorns education despite Ray Fairfax's only Albion goal.

It was to be the late 1970s when Albion next rubbed shoulders with clubs from mainland Europe – and that after a side fashioned by Johnny Giles and attractively improved by Ron Atkinson had finished sixth in the top flight in 1977-78.

Galatasary have latterly become well-known opponents in Europe, especially for Manchester United, but the Turks were fairly easy prey 20 years ago and Albion followed up a 3-1 win in Izmir by running out victors by the same score in the return, Laurie Cunningham and Bryan Robson featuring among the scorers each time.

Portugal was the next destination for Atkinson's talented squad and again they did the hard work on their travels, beating Sporting Braga 2-0 with a brace from Cyrille Regis and underlining their victory back on home soil with an Alistair Brown goal that saw them through 3-0.

Valencia in round four looked a daunting challenge,

complete as they were with Mario Kempes, an Argentinian World Cup-winning star of a few months earlier, and West German international Rainer Bonhof. But Albion performed brilliantly in the Luis Casanova Stadium and Cunningham's equaliser early in the second half earned his side a 1-1 draw and himself a £995,000 move to Real Madrid the following summer. The task was still only half

A mouthful of ball for Tony Brown as he runs into a clearance from the Portuguese 'keeper during Albion's second-leg 1-0 victory over Braga in the third round of the UEFA Cup. Ally Brown, also pictured, scored the goal that sealed a 3-0 aggregate success.

done but Albion again shone in the return and two goals from Tony Brown completed a memorable triumph.

Interest was high as Atkinson and his troops set off for the quarter-final against Red Star Belgrade at a time when they were also challenging Liverpool for the First Division championship. It took an 85th minute free-kick from the home side to break the deadlock in the first leg and there

My ball! It's almost like the bull and the matador as Tony Godden appears to be taunting the grounded Mario Kempes. Godden made 329 Albion appearances from 1977 to 1986 and set a club record in October, 1981, when he played in his 228th consecutive first-team game.

In control. John Wile and a fresh-faced Bryan Robson repel a Valencia attack in Spain in the first leg of the UEFA Cup fourth round. On the left is home striker Mario Kempes, one of the driving forces behind Argentina's lifting of the World Cup a few months earlier. The outstanding Laurie Cunningham scored in a highly impressive draw in the Luis Casanova Stadium.

was heartbreak back at The Hawthorns when another late goal equalised Regis's strike and put the Yugoslavs through 2-1 on aggregate.

Atkinson was still in charge when Albion, again through their League placing, qualified for a UEFA Cup return a year later. But there was no happy experience this time as surprise defeats home and away against Carl Zeiss Jena ended their interest at the first hurdle. The sending-off of Ally Brown at The Hawthorns made elimination against the East Germans even more depressing.

And it was the same story for Ronnie Allen's side two years later as the Albion striker-turned-manager returned to the Zurich Grasshoppers ground at which he had made his England debut against Switzerland three decades earlier. Albion were well in contention after losing the away leg 1-0 in front of only 8,101 spectators but they collapsed disappointingly 3-1 at The Hawthorns a fortnight later.

It was to be the club's last European experience for a long time …

Challenging at the Top

Winter wonderland. Albion wore specially-designed 'snow boots' to help them to this emphatic New Year's Day 1979 victory over visiting Bristol City. The 3-1 victory came two days after Ron Atkinson's side's much-televised 5-3 win away to Manchester United.

Shooting for the top! Tony Brown leaves Norwich and former England midfielder Martin Peters in his wake and fires goalwards at Carrow Road on January 13, 1979. The 1-1 draw, secured by a Cyrille Regis goal, took Albion top of the pile in the championship race.

No way through for Tony Brown in the big top-two showdown on February 3. Keeper Ray Clemence and Alan Kennedy bar the route to goal in Liverpool's vital win and Albion, whose form had been electric for several months, subsequently lost their way in the second of two major breaks because of snow.

A goal for Ally at Anfield. But it's not all that it seems. The scorer is the grounded Brown, not the already-celebrating Robertson, whom Cyrille Regis is about to embrace.

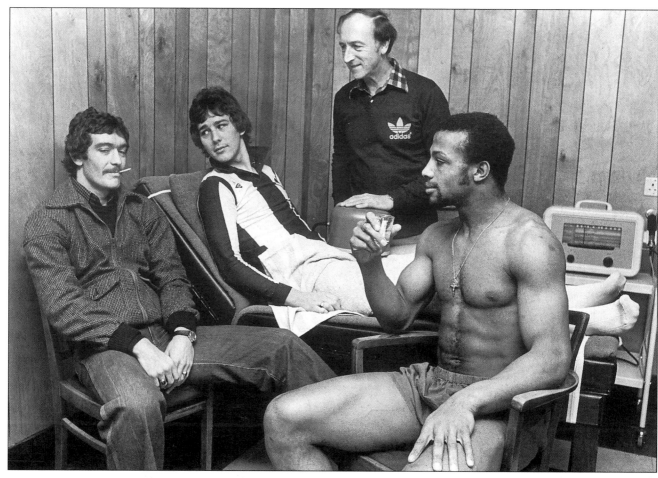

Hawthorns health check. Bryan Robson is on the couch for treatment on a groin strain, Cyrille Regis takes his medicine for a cold and Alistair Brown gets in on the act by taking his temperature under the watchful eye of physio George Wright on the eve of the resumption of Albion's European adventure.

And a quick word for the local media …Cyrille Regis, Laurie Cunningham and John Wile find themselves on duty in front of the microphone after training at the Crvena Zvezda Stadium. The match, away to Red Star Belgrade, on March 7, 1979, was witnessed by a gate of 95,300 – the biggest ever to see Albion at a club ground.

Touchdown in Yugoslavia. Time for a 'pose' with two Aer Lingus stewardesses before Albion prepare for the serious business of tackling Red Star in the UEFA Cup quarter-final.

So close to a vital away goal. Bryan Robson launches a header towards the target in Albion's 1-0 first-leg defeat, which was secured by a free-kick five minutes from time. After levelling the tie through Cyrille Regis at The Hawthorns, Albion went out to a goal in the dying minutes.

Robson again in the thick of the action as he forces Derby central defender Roy McFarland to boot clear in the Hawthorns mud on March 26, 1979. Albion won 2-1 and were still in the title race.

Laurie on the right road! Cunningham cuts in on goal to worry Mike Lyons and the rest of the Everton defence in Albion's 1-0 victory on April 7. It was Albion's sixth League win in a row but the bubble was about to burst …

John Trewick heads over John Gregory in a Friday night derby at Villa Park to give Albion their 24th and final League win of their nearly-glorious 1978-79 campaign. Before falling away in a punishing run-in containing 17 games in less than two months, Atkinson's men had pushed champions Liverpool hard.

UEFA Cup qualification had again been secured, long before Albion took on and lost 1-0 at White Hart Lane to a Tottenham side containing Colin Lee (left). Albion, represented here by Ally Brown, had the additional disappointment of losing two points and second place at home to Nottingham Forest four nights later.

Wedding bells for a future England captain as Bryan Robson marries Great Barr girl Denise Brindley at the Wesley Chapel in High Street, West Bromwich in the summer of 1979. Among the well-wishers are Albion colleagues (from left) John Wile, John Trewick, Alistair Brown, Len Cantello, Alistair Robertson, George Wright (physio), David Stewart and Tony Brown.

A word in your ear, young man. Brian Clough congratulates 1979 Midland Footballer of the Year Tony Brown. 'Bomber,' who had won the award in 1969 and 1971, scored 14 goals in the campaign, including the ones with which he first equalled and then overtook Ronnie Allen as the club's all-time record League marksman.

Having had a disappointing pay-back after making £516,000 David Mills Britain's costliest footballer in January, 1979, Ron Atkinson tried again in the market the following summer. This time he splashed out £748,000 – by now only a club record – on Manchester City winger Peter Barnes, who was to finish his career with 22 full England caps.

Albion's 1979-80 campaign started poorly with a home draw with Derby, defeats at Manchester United and Liverpool and then this 5-1 Hawthorns beating by European Cup holders Nottingham Forest. Kevin Summerfield is grounded as he and Tony Brown challenge Kenny Burns.

Three very fine gentlemen of the noble English game! Tony Brown, John Wile and Alistair Robertson don appropriate gear as they pose for publicity shots in September, 1979, prior to a centenary match at West Bromwich's Dartmouth Park to mark Albion's 100 years in existence.

Sliding in. Ally Brown goes to ground as he moves in to halt Villa's Allan Evans during the goalless draw at Villa Park on October 13, 1979 at a time when the club's season was picking up.

After their Hawthorns hammering by Forest, Albion fared little better at the City Ground early in the New Year. Despite this promising shot from John Deehan and a goal by the in-support Cyrille Regis, they were beaten 3-1. The match was substitute Tony Brown's last in the League for Albion – on the ground where he had scored all four goals in a Second Division victory in 1974.

Getting airborne. Brendon Batson challenges 1971 FA Cup Final hero Charlie George in Albion's 1-1 First Division draw with Southampton at The Dell on March 1, 1980. Ron Atkinson's side finished the season in mid-table, having gone out of the UEFA Cup (to Carl Zeiss Jena) and the FA Cup at the first attempt.

Bye, bye Bomber! After a staggering 279 goals in a club record 730 appearances, Tony Brown said his farewells in 1980, not without a few tears among Hawthorns staff and supporters. He saw out his playing career with Torquay, Stafford Rangers, New England Teamen and Jacksonville Teamen, then had coaching spells with Albion and Birmingham. His last League start for Albion was at Ipswich, where he also made his senior debut in 1963 at the age of 17.

A team picture with a difference. Albion's photo-call prior to the start of 1980-81 was conducted against the backdrop of a major building development. The Hawthorns' main stand was in the throes of being replaced by an impressive new structure.

First game, first defeat. Remi Moses and Hawthorns-manager-to-be Brian Talbot are neck and neck in this exchange from Albion's opening-day 1-0 setback against Arsenal.

Anfield, a profitable hunting ground for Albion in the 1960s and the mid-1970s, was a graveyard for them – and many others – by the early 1980s! This 4-0 trouncing came on September 13, 1980, despite John Trewick winning this tussle with Liverpool and England right-back Phil Neal.

From the same hiding, Cyrille Regis finds himself well shackled by Alan Hansen as he tries to burst away down the right. Just the sort of defending the imperious Liverpool centre-half now loves to praise on Match of the Day!

Peter Barnes leaves the Crystal Palace defenders in his wake on Albion's autumn visit to Selhurst Park. The game was settled by a thumping late header from Cyrille Regis, who was quickly descended upon by Brendon Batson and Alistair Brown (above).

Another Hawthorns hiding for Manchester United! This one came to the tune of 3-1 on December 27, 1980, and was a particularly significant one for the two Albion players pictured here with Sammy McIlroy. Peter Barnes had made his name with United's rivals City while Remi Moses later moved to Old Trafford, where he linked up again with Ron Atkinson and Bryan Robson.

Ally Brown on the prowl back at his former stamping ground. The Scottish striker was transferred to Albion from Leicester in 1972 and, approaching a decade later, was back at Filbert Street for this 2-0 League victory on January 10, 1981.

After their anti-climatic 1979-80, Albion were in a promising First Division position going into the final three months of the following campaign. John Deehan is pictured here during a 2-0 Valentine's Day win at Norwich that provided his side with their fifth victory in six League matches.

This is a hard hat area. Brendon Batson and John Wile pose as workmen as The Hawthorns continues to undergo its new look during 1980-81.

Almost good enough to put a spoke in Villa's wheel. Albion gave a good account of themselves on derby night in April, 1981, and this first-half Cyrille Regis header was one of many efforts on Jimmy Rimmer's goal. But Villa pinched a late winner and lifted the title a few weeks later.

Albion, having finished fourth in 1980-81 to again qualify for Europe, lost Ron Atkinson to Manchester United in the summer of 1981. Under Ronnie Allen, they kicked off two months later with a 2-1 defeat at Manchester City, where the long left leg of defender Tommy Caton was enough to halt John Deehan's progress.

City Ground flare-up! Fiery Scot Kenny Burns needs a restraining arm from Brendon Batson to prevent him clashing dangerously with Cyrille Regis during Albion's 0-0 draw at Nottingham Forest on September 12, 1981.

All smiles from Ronnie Allen on his return to the Zurich Grasshoppers ground where he made his England debut in 1952. But this trip to Switzerland was an unhappy one, Albion losing 1-0 in the first leg of the UEFA Cup first round and then being beaten 3-1 in the return – their last European tie.

This 1-0 Albion defeat at Everton, featuring a close-range miss by David Mills under the eye of former Goodison Park favourite Andy King, was another landmark occasion for the club. It was Bryan Robson's last game prior to his and Remi Moses's move to Manchester United for a then British record £2m. Robson played 249 games and scored 46 goals for Albion, for whom he once had the misfortune to break his leg three times in a year.

The sprint is on. Alistair Brown and Kevan Broadhurst are side by side as Colin Todd looks on from a safe distance at St Andrew's on October 31, 1981. An extraordinary game was highlighted by a Cyrille Regis hat-trick – and an Albion throwaway that allowed Birmingham to hit back and draw 3-3.

Brown again, forcing a cry of anguish from Tottenham 'keeper Ray Clemence as his shot is deflected into the net by Chris Hughton – one of Albion's goals in a 2-1 White Hart Lane triumph on November 7, 1981.

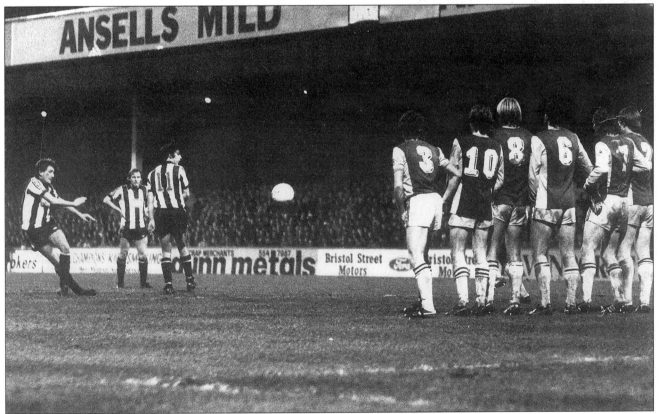

Albion were destined to finish down in 17th place in 1981-82 but their cup fortunes were a case of so near, so far. This 1-0 League Cup win at Villa, secured by Derek Statham's goal, put them in the semi-final. Gary Owen is the player trying his luck from a free-kick.

Semi-final letdown part one. Owen is again the central character as he emerges from a challenge by Ossie Ardiles, with Glenn Hoddle and Steve Perryman queuing up to confront him in the semi-final first leg at The Hawthorns.

A tense showdown, watched by a crowd of 32,166, became harder still when Dutch midfield hard-man Martin Jol was sent off in the second half for a second booking. Spurs' Tony Galvin was also dismissed. The game finished goalless.

At White Hart Lane a week later on February 10, 1982, Albion toiled hard – to no avail. Derek Statham was energetic enough to leave Ardiles in his slipstream but FA Cup holders Spurs won 1-0 with a 56th minute goal from Micky Hazard. On their way to the semi, Albion had beaten Shrewsbury, West Ham and Crystal Palace as well as Villa, being drawn away each time.

Out of the League Cup, Albion turned their sights to the FA Cup and savoured this 2-0 home win over Coventry in the quarter-final on March 6. A vintage Regis strike put Albion on their way before Gary Owen jumped high to celebrate his scoring of the side's second.

Back to Highbury four years on, this time to face Second Division QPR. Tony Currie looks on as Cyrille Regis does aerial battle with ex-Wolves defender Bob Hazell.

An occasion for the masses. Albion fans queue in their thousands for tickets after semi-final fever had again gripped The Hawthorns in the spring. The newspaper headline tells the story of Argentina's impending invasion of the Falkland Islands.

Painful business for a grounded John Wile. In front of hundreds of anxious pairs of eyes, he appears in immediate danger from a stray boot as he, Romeo Zondervan and Alistair Robertson battle to quell a Rangers attack.

Steve MacKenzie tries to weave his way through the QPR defence, with Tony Currie (left) and Gary Micklewhite in opposition and Derek Statham as support.

Semi-final letdown part two. Andy King was in need of attention on this occasion but his posture told a familiar depressing story. Albion were well and truly down and out, beaten by a freak second-half goal. Rangers lost to Tottenham in the Final, although Ardiles and Ricky Villa were absent because of the Falklands conflict.

The relief of it! Manager Ronnie Allen and full-back Derek Statham thank Albion supporters for their backing following a crucial late-season 2-1 victory at Notts County. Sidetracked by two long cup runs, Albion had lurched into relegation danger but ensured their survival three nights later by recording the win that sent Leeds down instead.

Off on the wrong foot again. For the third successive season, Albion kicked off in 1982-83 with a defeat, this one by 2-0 at Anfield. Debutant striker Peter Eastoe tries to break Liverpool's stranglehold with this shot past Phil Neal. Albion also lost their first match of the following two campaigns.

Hand in hand go Manchester United defender Mike Duxbury and Albion striker Ally Brown at The Hawthorns on September 4, 1982. Arthur Albiston, later to play for Albion, is the bystander as the Baggies, now under Ron Wylie following the summer departure of Ronnie Allen, beat United in this fixture (by 3-1) for an astonishing sixth time in seven years.

Ally on the warpath again! The goal-hungry striker is halted by the joint attentions of Arsenal 'keeper George Wood and defender David O'Leary in Albion's 2-0 League defeat at Highbury on October 16, 1982.

Paul Walsh beware! Martin Jol is launching himself into a determined tackle in Albion's 1-0 autumn victory at home to Luton – one that kept them, like their Dutch signing, flying high.

A derby-day goal for Albion's Peter Eastoe at the expense of 'keeper Tony Coton at St Andrew's on November 6, 1982. But the goal, watched by Pat Van Den Hauwe and Martyn Bennett, failed to save Albion from a 2-1 defeat.

Eastoe again has his sights on goal, this time with a fierce rising shot that gave Manchester United defender Gordon McQueen no chance of an interception. But Albion and United drew a blank in this First Division Old Trafford draw on January 3, 1983.

End of the line. Ally Brown is denied by Nottingham Forest 'keeper Steve Sutton in the 0-0 League draw at the City Ground on February 19, 1983 – his 359th and last game for Albion, for whom he scored 85 goals. In the distant background is John Wile, who was to leave at the end of the season after a magnificent 13-year stay containing 619 senior appearances and no fewer than seven ever-present League campaigns.

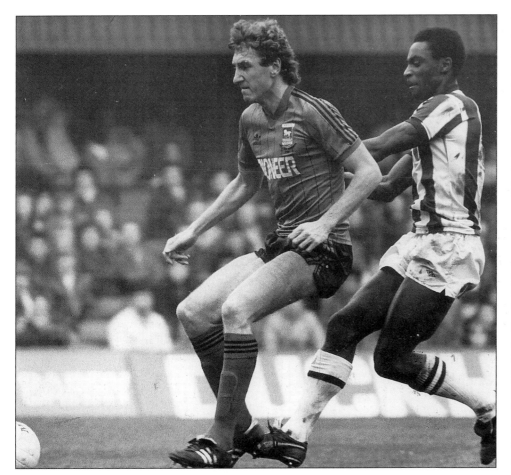

Garry Thompson turns up the heat on England central defender Terry Butcher in Albion's 4-1 Hawthorns triumph over Ipswich on March 12, 1983. Thompson, signed shortly before from Coventry, scored twice and averaged almost a goal every two games for the club in just over 100 outings.

A trophy to savour! Albion's youngsters, including Mark Grew, Mickey Lewis, Jan Webb, Gary Robson, Barry Cowdrill and Gary Childs, celebrate the winning of the Central League title in 1982-83 before going off to compete in a tournament in West Germany. Also pictured are director Cliff Edwards (left) and coach Albert McPherson.

Falling From Grace...

Through to the next round of the Milk Cup by piggy-back! Clive Whitehead hitches a ride with Cyrille Regis after the striker had scored one of his two goals in a 5-1 second-leg home win over Millwall in the second round of the 1983-84 competition. It was a spectacular night for Albion as they overturned a 3-0 first-leg deficit.

Following a 1-0 third-round win at Chelsea, Albion came to the end of the Milk Cup road with this 2-1 home defeat against Villa (left), despite this victory for Martin Jol in a midfield battle with Dennis Mortimer.

Derek Monaghan gets horizontal during Albion's 1-0 First Division triumph at Highbury on December 3, 1983. Looking on are Arsenal's Paul Davis and debutant Albion defender Michael Forsyth. This was the last win of the Ron Wylie reign. He departed ten days later.

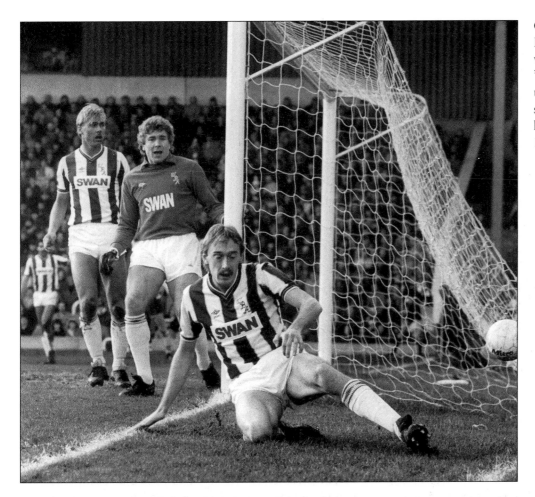

Close call! A sliding Barry Cowdrill, together with Martyn Bennett and 'keeper Paul Barron, ushers a Villa effort to safety during Albion's 3-1 home victory on January 14, 1984.

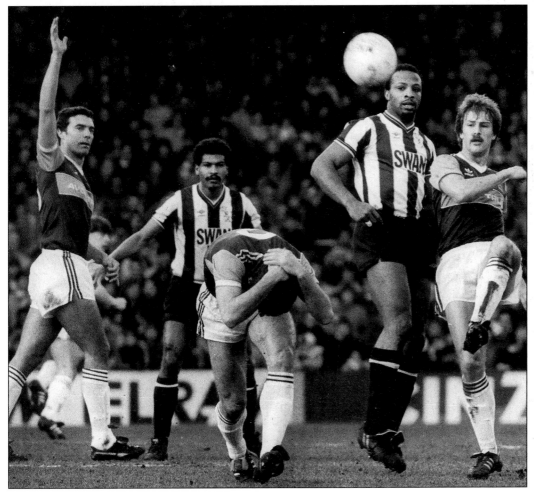

Back to London a month following the Highbury game, this time for a 1-0 League defeat at West Ham. Trevor Brooking appeals, a team-mate ducks, Romeo Zondervan and Cyrille Regis stand by and Neil Orr clears.

Joy for Noel Luke and Ken McNaught as they celebrate Micky Forysth's winner over visiting Scunthorpe in the fourth round of the FA Cup in February, 1984. Albion had put out another lower-division club, Rotherham, in round three.

He's back! Johnny Giles preaches his message as he talks Albion players through an early training session following his reappointment as manager in February, 1984. His second reign started sadly with a 1-0 home defeat against Plymouth in the FA Cup fifth round.

Football's plastic age (right). The studless footwear of QPR's Terry Fenwick and Albion goalscorer Garry Thompson bring home the vagaries of the Loftus Road pitch in the early 1980s. In the background in this May Bank Holiday 1-1 draw in 1983-84 is Tony Morley.

Mac the knife! Manchester United left-back Arthur Albiston – later of Albion – and centre-half Kevin Moran are powerless to stop Steve Mackenzie scoring one of the goals which gave Albion a fine 2-0 home win over the Reds in March, 1984 in the opening weeks of Johnny Giles's second spell as Hawthorns boss. This still stands as Albion's last win over a world-famous club who they beat memorably on many occasions in the 1960s, 1970s and early 1980s.

Classic style from midfielder Steve Hunt as he dives to head home Albion's first goal in the 4-0 trouncing of visiting Luton in September, 1984. But these were by no means boom-times for the club – note the empty seats. Despite this being the first Saturday home game of the season, only 11,720 were present – and a mere 13,464 had watched the midweek Hawthorns success over Everton.

A point from Anfield. Nicky Cross surges between Alan Kennedy and Mark Lawrenson in this goalless draw on October 6, 1984. Liverpool were European Cup holders at the time.

A trip to the unknown. Steve Hunt challenges for a high ball in a 0-0 Milk Cup draw at Wigan early in 1984-85. Hunt and the also-pictured Garry Thompson scored to help give Albion a 3-1 second-leg triumph.

Sky Blues put to the sword. Republic of Ireland midfielder Tony Grealish becomes one of five different Albion scorers – this was the side's fourth goal – in a 5-2 rout of Coventry on November 24, 1984.

Hawthorns comic capers! Micky Forsyth swings his left foot, a Watford defender looks away and Carl Valentine takes unnecessary evasive action in Albion's 2-1 win – their fifth victory in six First Division games up to the start of December, 1984.

Welcome to the New Year! Colin Gibson's right boot propels Aston Villa's first goal between Clive Whitehead and Martyn Bennett and puts Albion on course for a 3-1 defeat away to their big rivals on January 1, 1985.

A frank exchange of Old Trafford views between Gordon Strachan and Tony Grealish, with Garry Thompson having his say as well. On the far right is Manchester United's former Albion midfielder Remi Moses. The game was on February 2, 1985, and was won 2-0 by United.

A ding-dong at The Dell! David Cross, in his second Hawthorns spell, tussles with Kevin Bond on a late winter's day in 1985 on which Albion put three past Peter Shilton. Unfortunately, Tony Godden was beaten four times at the other end.

Hans Segers's athletic tip-over denies Nicky Cross on this occasion but the striker and Gary Owen were on target in Albion's 2-1 win at Nottingham Forest on March 16, 1985.

By hook or by Crooks. Ipswich defender Ian Cranson challenges Garth Crooks during a 2-1 Albion defeat in September, 1985, in which the former Tottenham and Stoke striker – and BBC reporter-to-be – scored a consolation goal.

World superstar meets long-serving Hawthorns hard-man. Bryan Robson appears to be getting a boot up the backside from Alistair Robertson – loyal veteran of 626 Albion games – in Manchester United's 5-1 First Division away win in September, 1985. Within a fortnight, Johnny Giles had resigned as Albion boss.

St Andrew's snow-bath. Steve Hunt slides in on Wayne Clarke as Mickey Thomas, Carlton Palmer, Martyn Bennett and Jimmy Nicholl look on during Albion's 1-0 February victory – their last match under the caretaker management of Nobby Stiles.

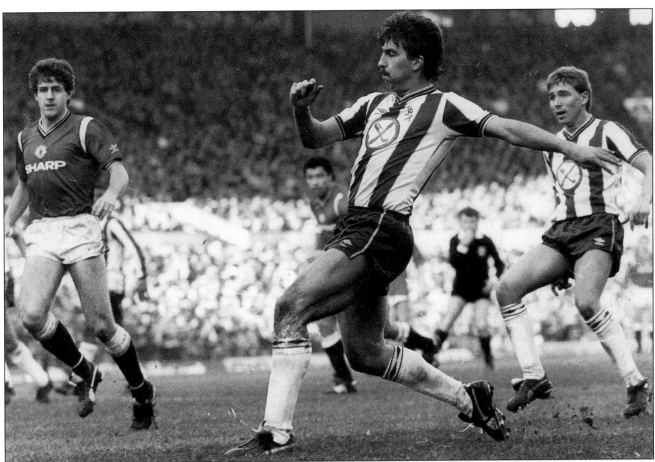

No way through! Ron Saunders's first League match as Albion manager ended in this 3-0 defeat at Manchester United on February 22, 1986. Gary Robson (right) and Colin Gibson watch as Steve Mackenzie plays a ball goalwards.

A Hawthorns point-saver from Martyn Bennett (No 6) against Nottingham Forest in the spring of 1986. George Reilly, Paul Dyson and a joyous Carlton Palmer were other members of Albion's sliding team while a young Des Walker is among the disbelieving Forest defenders.

The day relegation from the top flight became a mathematical certainty. A 1-0 defeat at QPR on April 12, 1986, confirmed what Albion fans had feared since their side went bottom of the table after three matches – and stayed there. Here, Paul Dyson tries a header at Rangers' goal watched by No 12 Steve Bull. It was a nightmare campaign in every way as Albion recorded a host of unwanted club records – only four League wins, suffering 26 defeats, mustering only 24 points from 42 games, losing nine successive League matches and using 34 players.

Gary Bannister, who sealed Albion's fate with the winner at Loftus Road and later moved to The Hawthorns, takes a tumble as Andy Thompson and Paul Dyson converge.

Clash of the volatile! Robert Hopkins skips over Stoke's Tony Kelly – later to become his Hawthorns team-mate – as Ron Saunders's Albion race to a 4-1 win over Stoke on Valentine's Day, 1987.

Doing battle in Albion's 0-0 second-leg draw against Walsall at Fellows Park in the first round of the 1987-88 Littlewoods League Cup is Martin Dickinson. Almost grounded is Saddlers striker David Kelly while David Burrows and Mark Goodwin hover. Walsall won 3-2 on aggregate and were promoted to the Second Division at the end of the campaign.

Getting the Wimbledon treatment! Bobby Williamson confronts Clive Goodyear in a 4-1 FA Cup third-round defeat away to the eventual Wembley winners in January, 1988. In five successive years, Albion went out of the Cup at their first hurdle – a miserable run ended when they beat Wimbledon 2-0 at The Hawthorns in 1989-90.

No contest! Tony Cascarino is head and shoulders above George Reilly in Millwall's 2-0 win over Albion at The Den on September 26, 1987. The defeat provided a reminder to new manager Ron Atkinson – appointed three weeks earlier – that he had inherited a much poorer team than the one he took over in the late 1970s.

Famous face in an unfamiliar kit (left). Andy Gray, taken to The Hawthorns during Ron Atkinson's second spell as manager, does aerial battle with David Linighan in Albion's 1-0 win at Shrewsbury in February, 1988.

Depressed times at the end of a troubled 1987-88 campaign. Watched by a crowd of only 8,004, Paul Dyson launches himself full length and heads Albion's goal in their 1-1 draw against Hull.

Not what it appears! It looks a goal, especially judging by the expressions of Don Goodman and Colin Anderson, but Walsall 'keeper Fred Barber and centre-half Graeme Forbes clear from under the bar and their side escape with a point from a 0-0 Hawthorns draw in the opening weeks of 1988-89.

The job is yours! Ron Atkinson's controversial walk-out for Athletico Madrid meant another change of manager at Albion, who appointed midfielder Brian Talbot, initially as caretaker, before this 4-1 victory at Birmingham in October, 1988.

The early weeks of Talbot's managerial reign were highly encouraging as Albion briefly went top of the Second Division in mid-season. Here, Don Goodman puts Cliff Carr to the sword before scoring his second goal in the 6-0 Hawthorns slaughter of a Stoke side later to emerge as a major bogey team to them.

Neighbourly combat. Darren Bradley, later to become a Walsall player, challenges Willie Naughton in Albion's 0-0 Second Division draw at Fellows Park on April Fool's Day, 1989. Albion missed out on the promotion play-offs.

Chris Whyte meets his captaincy counterpart from Vasco de Gama during Albion's end-of-season tour to America. Whyte scored in this 4-2 defeat in the San Jose Cup clash in California, Brian Talbot's side having crashed 6-1 to Real Madrid two days earlier.

Conga-time at The Hawthorns as Gary Robson, Kevin Bartlett, Adrian Foster, Chris Whyte and Colin West are joined by their Oldham counterparts in a 2-2 Second Division home draw on February 3, 1990.

The makings of a relegation season. Gary Bannister is pipped to a loose ball by Brighton 'keeper Perry Digweed, who was beaten only by a Steve Gatting own goal in this 1-1 Hawthorns draw in October, 1990.

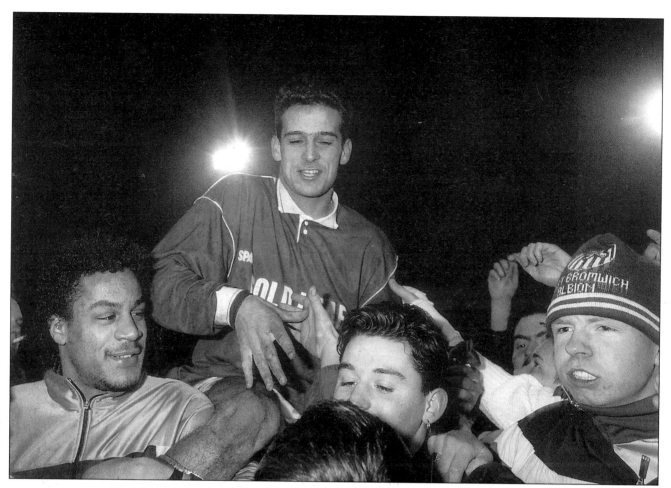

A Hawthorns hero but, sadly, not for Albion. Disillusioned home supporters join in the celebrations as Tim Buzaglo is chaired off following his hat-trick for non-League Woking in their 4-2 FA Cup third-round win in January, 1991. It was a humiliation that ended the 27-month reign as Albion boss of Brian Talbot.

The face of relegation. Tears flow from the eyes of supporter Teresa Hill after a last-day 1-1 draw against Bristol Rovers at Twerton Park in May, 1991, had failed to prevent Albion slipping into the Third Division for the first time in their 112-year history. The appointment of Bobby Gould as Talbot's replacement had brought an improvement – Albion were unbeaten in their final nine matches – but not enough of one. This picture was subsequently put on display to the players at The Hawthorns to remind them how much their fortunes meant to the fans.

Eccentric management ways. Reporters – and even a supporter on one occasion following a defeat at Bournemouth – couldn't believe their luck when Bobby Gould allowed them into Albion's dressing-room before and after games to quiz players. Among the beneficiaries here before a home victory over Stockport in the autumn of 1991 are John Bastow (Beacon Radio), Tim Beech (Radio WM) and the *Express & Star's* Denis Sunley.

Promotion at the first opportunity looked probable when Albion defeated Birmingham 3-0 on February 8, 1992. No 8 Bob Taylor, apparently about to be karate-chopped by Nigel Gleghorn, scored twice at St Andrew's but the team's promise didn't last.

How the mighty can fall! Albion, former Football League champions, five-times FA Cup winners and UEFA Cup quarter-finalists just over a decade before this picture was taken in March, 1992, have endured some hard times since last playing top-flight football. Here, they are not only playing Hartlepool at The Hawthorns in the League, but losing to them 2-1 despite the efforts of striker Gary Bannister.

The end is near …Albion fans make their feelings clear towards manager Bobby Gould at Shrewsbury on the final day of the 1991-92 season. Albion won 3-1 but, three days later, Gould was gone.

On the Way Back?

New face in town …Ossie Ardiles chats to Paul Raven, Bob Taylor, Colin West, Craig Shakespeare, Gary Hackett and Wayne Fereday shortly after his appointment as Albion manager in May, 1992.

Serial graffiti! For many years, the words 'Astle is the King' stood as tribute to Albion's 1968 FA Cup Final winner on this canal bridge in Netherton, near Dudley. It was washed off by Dudley Council in 1993 but reappeared almost immediately with the rider 'Please note, Dudley Council.' The repainted message prompted Dudley Council spokeswoman Mrs Alida Tricker to say: "Perhaps the slogan is like the White Horse and part of the natural landscape."

Bob Taylor was Bobby Gould's best Albion legacy and remained seated to celebrate this goal in a televised 2-2 FA Cup second-round draw at Wycombe in December, 1992. Albion, who had Simon Garner at No 7, won the replay 1-0 before losing at home to West Ham in round three.

Play-off action from Albion's first-leg trip to Swansea at the end of Ossie Ardiles's only season in charge. Bob Taylor, who finished this 1992-93 campaign with 37 goals – third behind WG Richardson (40) and Jimmy Cookson (38) in the club's list for goals in a season – harasses a defender on a day Albion needed an own goal to keep their deficit down to 2-1.

Bernard McNally is chaired off after it all came right in the second leg on May 19 with a 2-0 win and a 3-2 aggregate success. Goals from Andy Hunt and Ian Hamilton sent Albion to Wembley for the first time in more than 23 years.

Didn't we do well! From left, Paul Raven, Ian Hamilton, Bob Taylor and Ardiles's £100,000 signing Andy Hunt toast victory in the play-off semi-final.

On to the Final on May 30, 1993 – and more success! Andy Hunt lashes a shot goalwards despite the attention of Port Vale defender Dean Glover.

Yes! Hunt is all smiles after opening the scoring in the 65th minute in front of a crowd of 53,471 that contained an estimated 41,000 Albion supporters.

Goal number two nestles in the net from defender and man-of-the-match Nicky Reid's trusty right boot in the 80th minute. Paul Musselwhite is the helpless 'keeper.

And that rounds things off nicely. Kevin Donovan leaves Glover trailing and slots past Musselwhite to complete Albion's emphatic 3-0 victory in the last minute. It clinched promotion at the second time of asking from the (new) Second Division.

Albion's joyous homecoming was witnessed by tens of thousands of fans back in West Bromwich, where Bernard McNally was among those to take his salute.

Pre-season 1993. Who's that about to challenge Kevin Donovan? Glenn Hoddle was at The Hawthorns in Chelsea's line-up, with Kieran O'Regan to the left. Ossie Ardiles had stunned the club in June by walking out to rejoin Tottenham.

Donovan (left), later to get on the score-sheet himself, and Hunt (far right) display different reactions as Paul Raven screams his delight at his headed equaliser in the televised 3-2 Hawthorns victory over Wolves in September, 1993. Keith Burkinshaw's Albion side also won at Molineux, this time by 2-1.

How important those six points off Wolves were became evident at the end of the season as Albion survived by the skin of their teeth. Lee Ashcroft was the saviour with this last-day winner at Portsmouth on May 8, 1994, as the Baggies stayed up and Birmingham went down.

Survival is ensured and Albion fans are relieved to the point of needing to kiss the Fratton Park pitch.

End of an era. Down comes the Birmingham Road End in the summer of 1994 in preparation for an all-seater stand in accordance with the Taylor Report. The Woodman Corner, complete with scoreboard and throstle, has gone, too, along with the pitch!

Towards a New Millennium

WEST Bromwich Albion are a club steeped in proud tradition. They are also one with a changing face.

Redeveloped ground, new constitution with plc, exciting young players – and a new-generation support that boomed during the boing-boing promotion days of the early 1990s.

Popular and long-serving former skipper John Wile returned to Albion in 1997 in the new post of chief executive, hoping to oversee the push to bring the club up to Premiership standard on and off the pitch.

And, when the club celebrate 100 years at The Hawthorns in September, 2000, they aim to do so as a top-flight outfit – a first-class team in a first-class ground that has undergone major changes in recent years.

Gone is the decades-old structure that served as the 'home' Birmingham Road End of The Hawthorns. In its place since the mid-1990s is a towering new stand that Albion's most vocal supporters now populate.

Gone, too, is the old Smethwick End cover that had stood for even longer. That came down slightly earlier and has been replaced for the comfort of home and away fans.

The fans of tomorrow. The boing-boing spirit of The Hawthorns in the mid-1990s is captured delightfully by young Baggies supporters Darren Martin and Stephani Asbury. The duo, then four, are pictured at a 'photo-call' at Guns Village Infants School in West Bromwich.

The first half of a memorable double Albion triumph over neighbours Wolves in 1997-98. Alan Miller joined in the Ravanelli craze to celebrate this 1-0 Sunday lunchtime Hawthorns success in late August, sealed by a bizarre own-goal from Wolves skipper Keith Curle.

It's now nearly 20 years since the main stand on the Halfords Lane side of the ground was demolished in favour of the modern structure that houses the dressing-rooms, VIP lounges, directors' box, boardroom, media areas and hospitality boxes.

Now, there are plans to send the bulldozers in on the Rainbow Stand opposite and turn an already impressive stadium into one for supporters to be really proud of.

Behind the scenes, too, the times have changed. In a bid to create greater finances for new players, the club joined the fashion for going public and so started to dismantle an archaic constitution.

Sheffield businessman Paul Thompson was a major player in the transition, with hard-working and ambitious chairman Tony Hale determined that the money-raising efforts should be a springboard for challenging hard for promotion.

By the summer of 1998, Albion had already been out of the top flight for 12 years – quite long enough for a club who were founder members of the Football League in 1888 and who have won the FA Cup five times, the League Championship once and the League Cup once.

The club had 24 years of unbroken membership of the top flight from 1949 to 1973 – one of the longest in the country at that time – and their Cup-fighting qualities became legendary in that period.

For young and old fans alike, the return to those dizzy heights can't come a day too soon.

Subscribers

Bryan R Adams
David Adams
Dylan J Adams
J B Adams
Roger, Kim and Matthew Adams
David Ager
John Aldridge
Malcolm Richard Alexander
David Joseph Allcock
John Scott Allen
Mr William H Allen
Robert Amphlett
Bill Andrews Jnr
Mr Thomas Reuben Andrews
Michael David Anstis
Nicolas John Archer
David Ashford
Mr G K Ashman
Mr G Ashmore
Lisa Astbury
J K Aston
Mrs Lily Aston
Robert Wayne Atkins
Gary Attwood
Mr Graham Auliffe
John Albert Bailey
Mr Brian Baker
Joseph Baker
Steve Baker
Andrew N Ball
John Ball
Simon Ballinger
Hazel M Banks
Martin Banner
James Barber
Steve Barber
Gillian Barker
Paul Barker
J D Barlow
John Barlow
L & J M Barnsley
Thomas Wilson Barrett
Gary Barton
Robert Barton
Mrs S E Basford
Ronald Bate
Paul Andrew Bates
Dr John Batham
Craig A Beale
Julie A Beale
Michael Beard
Steve Beard
Andrew F Beckley
Stephen Beddard
Don Bedlow
R J Bedward
Roy Belcher
Carlton D Bell
Graham Bell
Derek Berry

Mr Jan Bibilo
Lee Biddle
Gareth Biggs
Deborah Birch
P J Bird
Mr P K Birdi
G L Blackham
Ian Blackham
Mr T H Blower
Thomas Blundell
William Blunt
Miss Susan C Board
James Boden
A A Boffy
Peter J Bond
Peter Bone
David Botfield
Benjamin Bott
Mr G A Bowen
Matthew Bradley
Adrian Bradley
Robert S Bradley
Robin O Bragg
Miss Sharon Brain
Mr Robert and Mr David Bridge
Mr Anthony Bridgewater
Paul Andrew Brindley
Mrs E S Bromley
Mr C R Brookes
M H Brookes
Ron Brookes
Douglas Brown
Michael John Brown
Paul Brown
Philip J Brown
Michael Bryan
Mick Bryan
Clive Buckland
R D Bull
Dr J Bullock
Stuart John Bullock
Christopher Bunce
David Burgess
Philip David Burgess
Simon Burgess
J T Burton
Mr Mark Butler
R J Bytheway
Bryan Caddick
Kevin Cadman
Mr P F Cain
J H Cammies
Daniel Carpenter
Stephen Carr
E Carter
Fred Carter
Ian M Cartwright
James Robert Cartwright
Christopher Cash
H B Cashmore

A Challis
Trevor Challoner
Stephen Chance
D Channings
Ben Chapman
Albert Chattin
Peter Chawner
A J Church
Brian Churchill
Michael John Churchill
Sid Clark
Ike Clarke – Ex WBA Player
Brian Clarke
Clive Clarke
Alan David Clarkson
Nicholas Clarkson
Philip Clements
Earl Cliff
Roger Cliff
James Howard Coates
Marion and John Cole
Martin Cole
Gordon Richard Coles
Richard Coles
D K Coley-Fisher
Jeremy James Cooke
Gordon Cooper
Darren Cooper
David Cooper
Geoff Cooper
J W Cooper
M Cooper
R J Cooper
William Cooper
Keith L Cope
J Corbett
Joe Cottam
Mr Jason Cox
Marc Cox
Peter Cox
Robert Neal Cox
David A Coy
Richard Cresswell
Timothy Cross
Russell John Crowe
Patrick Crowley
Adele Crump
Matthew Crumpton
James Cubitt
Phil Cummings
Mr Anthony Curtis
Andrew Cutler
Mr S Dalloway
James Dalton
Mr Joseph Dangerfield
A Darby
D R Darby
Neil Robert Darrock
Trevor Darrock
Nicholas Byrne

Richard Thomas Davenport
Andrew Davies
B A Davies
Colin Davies
I A Davies
Michael Davies
Michael Davies
Steven Davies
A P Davis
Anthony Davis
David Davis
Fred Davis
John Davis
Mr M J R Davis
Richard Davis
Gary B Day
Allen John Day
Michael Day
Mike Day
Peter John Dean
Alan and Sheila Deane
Mr Colin Debney
Mr Jonathan Deeley
Mark Philip Denning
David Derry
Geoffrey Dicken
Mrs F Dickinson
Philip Dieryck
David J Dimmock
Mr K Dodd
James Alexander Dolphin
M L Donovan
Jonathan Dowen
Stuart Raymond Down
Mr Kenneth Drury
Mr P Dubberley
Stephen Duckhouse
Tony Duncan
Gordon R Dunn
Tony Dunn
Trevor John Durden
Matthew Edwards
Roger Edwards
David Elcock
Mark Eley
Terence Michael Elkin
J A Elwell
Edgar Thomas Evans
Robert Paul Evans
William E Evans
Eddie Fallon
Nicholas Farley
Colin Fellows
R B Findlay
Steve Finn & Linda Millard
Keith Robert Fisher
Wayne Maurice Fisher
P R Fletcher
Katie Flower
Ray Forrest
John William Francis
Alan Graham Franks
Mrs Joan Freeman
Ken Freeman
Tony Freeman
Teresa Fryer
Lee Dean Fullwood

Noel Garbett
Leonard S Gardner
Henry Charles Garfield
Jeffrey Garland
Stan Garrett
John Gaskin
Darren Geddes
Mr M E Gerrard
Terence Gibbons
Kenneth Thomas Gibbs
Craig Anthony Gilder
Richard James Gilder
J W Glassey
Andrew Glazzard
Mr G P Glover
G I F Godby
I P F Godby
A Golcher
A T Gooding
Mr Norman Goring
John Gough
Philip Gough
Robert Gough
Ian Goulcher
Margaret Gould
Tony Goule
Ian Grainger
Jim Grainger
Paul Grainger
J L Green
G Grice
David Griffiths
David Griffiths
George Griffiths
Martin Griffiths
Mr R Griffiths
Stephen Griffiths
Stephen D Griffiths
Steve Griffiths
Steven Griffiths
Mr R S Grimes
Barry Guest
Darren John Gutteridge
Dave Hackett
Arthur Joseph Hadley
Frank Haffner
Mr Christopher W Hale
Ben Hall
Katrina Hall
Peter Hall
Mr W J Hall
Neil Hamilton
H Hancock
J Hancocks
Mowlah Hancox
W Ronald Hands
Robin H Harman
Michael D Harper
Lindsay Harpin
Len Harris
Mr Roger P Harris
Kevin Harrison
L H Harrison
William H Harrison
Mr Paul Hart
Michael John Harvey
Tim Haskey

Martin Hassell
Stuart Hatfield
Vincent Haughey
Mr R A Haycock
Mr Norman Hayden
Peter Hayes
Douglas Haynes
Laura Haynes
William Healey
Michael Heeley
Paul Hemming
Pamela Henderson
Matthew Hennefer
Roy Hennefer
Pete Henry
H A Heritage
Stephen Hevican
Mr J B Hickling
Mr W Hickman
Mrs G J Hill
Andrew Hill
Brian Hill
Michael Hill
Royston Brian Hill
W T Hill
Rob Hindley
Adam J R Hingley
Geoff Hingley
Paul Hiscock
Chris Hockell
Ivor J Hodgetts
Duncan Edward Hodgkiss
Mr D Holden
Anthony Holland
David Hollingmode
N H Hollis
Mark Holloway
James Holmes
Stuart Holmes
Chris Holt
F Homer
Ian Robert Homer
John Joseph Homer
Joseph Anthony Homer
Michael A Homer
P E Homer
Mr A Hope
Mrs Marian Horton
Robert Horton
F H Howell
Alan Hughes
Andrew Hughes
B J Hughes
Mr Barry Hughes
Gareth Hughes
George Hughes
Mr R J Hughes
Jonathan Hunt
Joseph Stanley Hunt
Lawson Hunt
Mr Leigh Hunt
Scott Innes
Gordon Inwood
Chris Jackson
D G Jackson
Dale Jackson
David Jackson

SUBSCRIBERS

Graham Jackson
Norman Jackson
Pauline A Jackson
Ronald Jarratt
Alan Jarvis
Mr V W Jarvis
Mr D J Jeavons
S M Jeens
Mr J Jeffcott
Albert E Jenks
Alan Jennings
Mark Jevons
K Johnson
Malcolm Jones
Mark Jones
Martyn A Jones
Mrs P Jones
P J Jones
Peter Jones
Roger Jones
Ronald P J Jones
Stephen Jones
Vera D Jones MBE
Andrew Jordan
Robert Judd
Adrian Kay
John Keay
George E Kemshall
Andrew George Kemshall
Mrs L Kendrick
Mr Alfred Leslie Kenny
Christopher Key
Robert Andrew Kings
Mike Kinson
Matthew J Knight
M M Knowles
Michael Knowles
Claude Laight
David Lane
Jonathan Lane
Martin Lane
Robert Langford
Phillip Edward Langley
Marc Leashorne
Robert Leatherland
Ian Lee
Tony Leeds
Alan J Lewis
Nigel George Lewis
Mark David Liddington
Charles Lilley
Ian Littlehales
Mr Spencer Lloyd
Nigel Long
Stephen Long
Mark Longdon
Ian Longmore
Mr Joseph W Lovell
C S Lowe
John Lowe
R D Lowe
Timothy McCarthy
John William McDonald
Robert James McDonald
Richard C Mace
Ross McElligott
Gavin McMail

Mr S G McNeil
Cathy Maddox
David Madelin
Mr A K Mall
Mr T B Mallin
Gordon Mansell
Paul Mansell
Mr J Margetts
Dean Marsh
Richard James Marsh
Adrian Marshall
Mrs V Martin
Alan Horace Mascall
Alan Masefield
Neil David Mason
Roy Henry Mason
Freda Matthews
Mr M Meacham
Philip Meadows
Keith L Melhuish
Vannessa Melia
Ken S Meredith
Brian Merritt
Mark Terence Miller
Paul John Mills
Robert Mills
Robert L Mills
Robert Whitelaw Mills
Thorne Mitchell
Ian Moczadlo
Stephen Mole
Eric S Moore
Helen Moore
Mrs J M Moore
June Moore
Thomas Moore
J W Moren
David E Morgan
Charles Morris
Emily Morris
Mr J R Morris
John Kenneth Morris
Paul Morris
Sarah Moseley
The Mottons
Derek James Mottram
Richard Mullen
Stephen John Murphy
Peter Nash
Norman Neal
Stuart Newton-Pepi
Matthew Nicholls
Richard Everton Nicholls
Ricky Nicholls
Kevin Nichols
Christopher Nock
Gemma Louise Nock
Andy and Daniel Norton
Mr Eric Norton
Chris O'Neill
George Oliver
Jamie John Oliver
Philip David Orme
Nathan James Painter
Douglas Parish
Geoff Parker
Ian Parkes

J Parkes
R Parkes
A E H Parsons
Andy Partridge
Andrew Patrick
Mr David Payne
John H Pearson
Jonathon A Pearson
M W Pedley
S Pedley
Kenneth Peel
Graham Peplow
Arthur Perry
Mr G J Perry
C J Phillips
Mike Phipps
Wayne Pickett
Mark Pilsbury
Andrew Piper
Brian A Pitt
N A Plant
Keith Plimmer
John Poole
Gary Porter
Denis John Portman
Glen Portman
Matthew Potter
Mr David Poulton
Stephen Povey
Malcolm John Powell
John Wesley Pratt
Vincent W Preece
K Preene
Chris Preston
Bill Price
Carl Price
S M Price
Graham Price
T J H Price
Michael F Priddy
David Priest
Chris Prinn
Michael Proctor
G E Pugh
Paul Ratcliffe
Mr Mark Raybould
John Henry Keith Read
A Reade
Mr M J F Reaney
Ron Rees
Reeve Family
John Reeves
Nick Reeves
Jonathan Reid
Noel Reilly
Paul David Render
Craig Reynolds
Mrs Olive Rhodes
Paul Rich
Ian G Riddell
William Roach
Christopher David Roberts
Clifford James Roberts
Maurice Roberts
Paul Roberts
Duncan Robinson
Ian James Robinson

Keith Robinson
Paul Robottom
Mr D N Rogers
M J Rolinson
Christopher John Rollings
Mr M J Rose
Malcolm Rose
Steve Rose
Michael Ross
A E Round
Martin Round
Mick Rowe
Milly E Rowe
David A Rowley
G A Rushton
C G Rymer
Mr W J Sabin
Gary Salt
E G Sanders
R J Sandford
Sandwell Community Libraries
Gareth David Sargeant
John E Saunders
John Farrington
M Screen
Bobby Senior
Paul Seymour
Philip Shaw
Edward Maurice Shelley
Frederick Eric Shelley
Mr M Shepherd
Paul James Shepherd
Ian Shermer
Andrew J Sidebotham
Elizabeth Sidwell
Mr Keith Siggins
Judy Simcox
Mr G A Simcox
Mr J R M Simcox
Bernard Simmonite
Mr F C Simms
Peter Sinar
Mazar Singh
Bob Skelding
David Skidmore
Mr Philip Skidmore
Alan Slater
James Slater
Andrew J Smith
Mr Barrie Smith
Christopher Smith
David Smith
Mr Denys A Smith
Graham Smith
J P Smith
J W Smith
Mr Kevin J Smith
P J Smith
Dale A B Smyth
Neal J B Smyth
Paul W B Smyth
Stephen Smytheman
Mrs S M Sorrill
Martyn Spink
C J Spruce
Leigh Sprules
Glyn D Stacey

W R Stallwood
A E Stanford
F Stanley
Paul N Startin
Michael Dennis Stevens
V Stevens
Ken Stockton
David Stokes
Errol F E Stokes
Mr Robert Stone
Chris Swallow
Laura, Jack and Sarah Swallow
Mark Swallow
Mrs P M Swann
David Swene
Gary G Talbot
Mark Talbot
Patrick Talbot
Philip Tandy
Alan Taylor
David Taylor
David John Taylor
Kenneth Taylor
Mark Garry Taylor
Martin Taylor
Peter A Taylor
Robert Taylor
Graham Thacker
M G Thomas
Mrs Anne Thompson
J H Tillson
William Timmington
B M Timmins
Bernard R Tonks
Tony Turner
Barbara Tout
Peter & Debbie Tovey
Brian Trevis
Brian Trevis
Andrew Trumper
Nicholas Trumper
Derek Tudor
Kenneth John Turley
Mr Adrian Turley
Alan W Turley
Bill Turner
Carl A Turner
Mr Frank Turner
Peter Turner
Sue Turner
J V Tuzzio
Thomas Tycer
Ron Upton
Mr Bogdan Vjestica
Brett Andrew Wain
Mrs J Waite
Malcolm Waite
Jeffrey J Wakelam
Grenville Durbin Wakeman
J L R Walker
John Beresford Walker
Morris Walker
N G Walker
Philip Walker
Ronald Walker
Ray Wallace
Ray Wallis

Mrs D Walsgrove
Mr Barry Walters
Stephen Walters
B R Want
Paul Want
Mr A B Ward
Andrew N Ward
Matthew Ward
Laurie Wassell
R L Watkins
Don Watson
Philip Robert Watson
Stuart Watson
David Watton
M E Watton
Mr K Welch
Ashley and Jamie Wesson
Kevin Westwood
Robert Wheeler
William George Wheeler
Andrew White
Brett White
Aaron Whitehead
Andrew / Geoffrey Whitehouse
Cliff Whitehouse
Dr Darren Whitehouse
Derek Whitehouse
Mark Whitehouse
Patrick J Whyte
Bennett Wilkes
C J Wilkes
George Henry Willetts
Stephen Willetts
Stuart M Willetts
Albert Williams
Kevin Alan Williams
Paul William Williams
Russell Williams
Simon John Williams
Stephen Williams
Stephen George Williams
Dr C J Wilson
David Wilson
Mark Wilson
Colin J Winchurch
Stephen Winston
Graham Withers
Ian Withers
K P Withnall
Stephen Wolff
Stuart D Wood
Reverend Roger Woodall
Stephen G F Woodall
Tom Woodbine
L H Woodhall
Jack Woodward
Miss C L Woolley
Barry M Woolridge
Keith Woolridge
Mr M W Worley
Robert Worley
Anthony Raynor Worton
C T Wright
Chris Wright
Paul Wright
Paul Wright
Sydney Wyatt